THE BOOK OF

GIFTS
From the Pantry

THE BOOK OF

GIFTS
From the Pantry

ANNETTE GRIMSDALE

Photography by RAY JOYCE

GUILD PUBLISHING
LONDON

This edition published 1987 by
Book Club Associates.
By arrangement with Salamander Books Limited and
Merehurst Press, London.

Editors: Susan Tomnay, Hilary Walden, Chris Fayers
Designers: Susan Kinealy, Roger Daniels, Richard Slater, Stuart Willard
Food stylist: Jan Barnett
Photographer: Ray Joyce
Typeset by Lineage
Colour separation by Fotographics Ltd, London–Hong Kong
Printed by New Interlitho S.p.A., Milan

Companion volumes of interest:
The Book of GARNISHES
The Book of COCKTAILS
The Book of CHOCOLATES & PETITS FOURS
The Book of HORS D'OEUVRES
The Book of SAUCES
The Book of ICE CREAMS AND SORBETS
The Book of PRESERVES

CONTENTS

INTRODUCTION 7
DRESSINGS, SAUCES & CONDIMENTS 8
SAVOURY PRESERVES 22
SNACKS 32
SWEET PRESERVES 60
DRINKS 74
SWEETS 78
BAKED GIFTS 100
ASSORTMENTS 120
INDEX 128

INTRODUCTION

'The art of giving presents is to give something
which others cannot buy for themselves.'
A. A. Milne.

This is a book of ideas for gifts that cannot be bought ready made in the shops. The gifts are more meaningful and therefore more welcome because of the love and thought that has gone into their preparation and into the boxing and wrapping of them. Many of these gifts will last, but some are to be eaten and enjoyed at once. Whichever type of recipe you choose for your friends or loved ones, I know they will be delighted to receive a gift uniquely yours. Happy giving!

BLUE CHEESE DRESSING

60g (2 oz) Roquefort or blue cheese, mashed
1 clove garlic, crushed
$\frac{1}{2}$ teaspoon dry mustard
1 egg yolk
2 tablespoons white wine vinegar
1 teaspoon salt
1 teaspoon sugar
$\frac{1}{2}$ teaspoon white pepper
125 ml (4 fl oz/$\frac{1}{2}$ cup) vegetable oil

In a bowl, mix together cheese, garlic, mustard and egg yolk.

Stir in vinegar, salt, sugar and pepper.

Stir in the oil drop by drop until half of oil has been added. Then stir in oil in a steady stream. Pour into clean container. Store in refrigerator. Will keep up to 2 weeks.

Makes about 250 ml (8fl oz/1 cup).

GREEN GODDESS DRESSING

2 anchovy fillets, drained, mashed to a paste
1 clove garlic
250 ml (8 fl oz/1 cup) Mayonnaise (see recipe page 10)
1 tablespoon lemon juice
1 tablespoon tarragon vinegar
2 tablespoons chopped parsley
60 ml (2 fl oz/¼ cup) sour cream
Salt and pepper
2 teaspoons fresh chopped tarragon or chives, if desired

Mix anchovies with garlic and Mayonnaise.

Stir in lemon juice, vinegar, onions and parsley.

Add sour cream and taste for salt and pepper. Sprinkle tarragon over top, if desired. Pour into clean container. Store in refrigerator. Will keep up to 7 days.

Makes about 440 ml (14 fl oz/1¾ cups).

MAYONNAISE

3 egg yolks, room temperature
Pinch of dry mustard
1/2 teaspoon salt
310 ml (10 fl oz/1 1/4 cups) olive oil, room temperature
1/2 teaspoon tarragon vinegar

In a medium-size bowl, combine egg yolks, mustard and salt.

Stirring with a wooden spoon, add olive oil drop by drop making sure that each drop has been absorbed before adding the next. When yolks start thickening, oil can be added in a thin stream, until a third of the oil has been incorporated. Add vinegar drop by drop, alternatively with remaining oil, until vinegar is incorporated.

Add any remaining oil very slowly stirring constantly. Pour into clean container, cover. Store in refrigerator up to 7 days.

Makes about 1 3/4 cups.

Spicy Barbecue Sauce

2 large onions, finely chopped
2 fresh chillies, finely chopped
3 cloves garlic, crushed
1 teaspoon dry mustard
1 teaspoon salt
2 teaspoons pepper
1 tablespoon brown sugar
250 ml (8 fl oz/1 cup) tomato ketchup
125 ml (4 fl oz/½ cup) olive oil
90 ml (3 fl oz/⅓ cup) lemon juice
2 tablespoons tarragon vinegar
1 tablespoon Tabasco sauce
2 tablespoons chilli sauce
125 ml (4 fl oz/½ cup) water

In a saucepan combine all ingredients except chillies.

Bring to a boil. Add chilies. Simmer 15 minutes.

Pour into sterilized jars to within ½ cm (¼ in) of top. Seal with sterilized vinegar-proof lids. Store in a cool, dark place.

Makes 750 ml (1¼ pt/3 cups).

SALSA BOLOGNESE

2 small onions, chopped
½ teaspoon dried oregano
1 stalk of celery, finely chopped
1 small carrot, finely chopped
60 ml (2 fl oz/¼ cup) corn oil
250 g (½ lb) lean minced beef
Salt and freshly ground pepper
Pinch of nutmeg
125 ml (4 fl oz/½ cup) dry white wine
250 ml (8 fl oz/1 cup) beef stock
2 tablespoons tomato paste

In a large heavy-bottomed saucepan or frying pan fry onion in oil 2 minutes; add celery and carrot, fry until soft. Add meat and brown thoroughly.

Add salt, pepper, nutmeg and oregano. Increase heat and add white wine. Bring to a boil and allow most of the wine to evaporate.

Add beef stock and tomato paste and simmer 30 to 45 minutes. Adjust seasoning if necessary. Pour sauce into jars, seal and cool. Store in refrigerator up to 7 days.

Makes about 750 ml (1¼ pt/3 cups).

CHILLI SAUCE

6 medium-size onions, finely chopped
125 ml (4 fl oz/½ cup) peanut oil
10 cloves garlic, chopped
1 small green pepper, chopped
2 tablespoons fresh grated ginger root
220 g (7 oz) fresh red chillis, chopped
375 ml (12 fl oz/1½ cups) tomato ketchup

In a large, heavy-bottomed saucepan or frying pan, gently fry onions in oil until they are soft.

Add pepper, garlic and ginger and cook two minutes more. Add chillies (leave all the seeds in if you want a very hot sauce; remove some or all for a milder sauce). Simmer for about 5 minutes.

In a food processor or blender, place mixture with tomato ketchup. Blend until mixture is a purée. Return to saucepan and simmer gently 15 minutes more. Pour into sterilized jars. Seal. Cool. Store in the refrigerator. Will keep up to 4 months.

Makes about 750 ml (1¼ pt/3 cups).

SALSA PIZZAIOLO
(NEAPOLITAN TOMATO SAUCE)

1 kg (2 lb.) fresh tomatoes
2 onions, finely chopped
2½ tablespoons corn oil
5 cloves garlic, finely chopped
185 g (6 oz) can tomato paste
¾ tablespoon chopped fresh oregano
¾ tablespoon chopped fresh basil
1 bay leaf
2 teaspoons sugar
Salt and fresh ground pepper

Peel, core and coarsely chop tomatoes.

In a large, heavy-bottomed saucepan fry onions in oil until soft.

Add garlic and cook another minute, stirring constantly (do not allow garlic to brown). Add tomatoes, tomato paste, oregano, basil, bay leaf, sugar, salt and pepper to saucepan. Bring to a boil over high heat; immediately reduce heat and simmer gently for about 30 minutes. Remove bay leaf and adjust seasoning if necessary. If you like a very smooth texture you can purée the sauce. Pour sauce into jars, seal. Store in refrigerator up to 10 days.

Makes about 1.5 l (2½ pt/6 cups).

TOMATO RELISH

1.5 kg (3 lb.) tomatoes
4 large onions, coarsely chopped
125 g (4 oz/¾ cup) salt
600 ml (1 pt/2 ½ cups) white wine vinegar
440 g (14 oz/1¾ cups) sugar
6—10 small red chillies
1 tablespoon curry powder
1 tablespoon turmeric
1 ½ teaspoons dry mustard
1 teaspoon cumin
1 teaspoon fenugreek
2 tablespoons plain flour

Peel, core and coarsely chop tomatoes.
Place in a ceramic or glass bowl, sprinkle
generously with salt; cover; let stand
overnight. In a large saucepan combine
tomatoes, onions and vinegar. Bring to
a boil; simmer 10 minutes. Add sugar
and chillies. Cook, stirring occasionally,
until sugar is dissolved. Simmer 5 minutes
more.

In a small bowl combine remaining
ingredients and enough cold water to
form a paste. Add to simmering
vegetable mixture, stirring to avoid any
lumps. Simmer 1½ hours stirring
occasionally.

Pour into sterilized jars. Seal with
sterilized vinegar-proof lids. Store in
cool, dark place – allow to mellow 4
weeks before using.

Makes about 1.9 l (3¼ pt/8 cups).

— GREEN PEPPERCORN MUSTARD —

6 tablespoons white mustard seeds
3 tablespoons green peppercorns
2 tablespoons honey
60 ml (2 fl oz/¼ cup) cider vinegar
1 tablespoon salt
½ teaspoon ground nutmeg
¼ teaspoon ground allspice

In a blender grind mustard seeds finely. In a glass or ceramic bowl, mix together mustard powder and 3 tablespoons water and let stand for 30 minutes.

In a blender place mustard mixture, green peppercorns, honey, vinegar, salt, nutmeg and allspice. Blend ingredients until mustard acquires a grainy texture. If mixture seems too dry, add a little more water or honey.

Cover and let stand 12 hours before pouring into sterilized jars. Seal. Store in a cool, dark place 2 weeks before using. Refrigerate after opening.

Makes about 250 ml (8 fl oz/1 cup).

HORSERADISH MUSTARD

60g (2 oz/¼ cup) dry mustard
2 tablespoons grated fresh horseradish
1 teaspoon salt
60 ml (2 fl oz/¼ cup) white vinegar
1 tablespoon olive oil

In a food processor or blender combine all ingredients.

Process until a smooth paste is formed.

Pour into sterilized jar and seal. Store in the refrigerator – allow to mellow 2 weeks before using.

Makes about 185 ml (6 fl oz/¾ cup).

— HOT MALT WHISKY MUSTARD —

60 g (2 oz/¼ cup) black mustard seeds
60 g (2 oz/¼ cup) yellow mustard seeds
4 tablespoons water
155 ml (5 fl oz/⅔ cup) cider vinegar
155 ml (5 fl oz/⅔ cup) whisky
125 ml (4 fl oz/½ cup) honey
1 tablespoon ground nutmeg
1 tablespoon salt
Add if a very grainy mustard is desired:
60g (2 oz/¼ cup) black mustard seeds
60g (2 oz/¼ cup) yellow mustard seeds

In a blender grind black and yellow mustard seeds.

In a glass or ceramic bowl mix together mustard powder and water, let stand 30 minutes.

Place mustard mixture, vinegar, whisky, honey, nutmeg and salt in blender or food processor. Process until mustard acquires a grainy texture. Add more honey if ingredients look too dry. Add additional whole black and yellow mustard seeds if desired. Blend again, breaking down grains but still retaining a 'whole grain' appearance. Cover; let stand overnight. Moisten with more honey if mixture appears too dry. Pour into sterilized jars and seal. Store in a cool, dark place – allow to mellow 3 weeks before using. Refrigerate after opening.

Makes 600 ml (1 pt/1½ cups).

MIXED HERB VINEGAR

60 g (2 oz/1 cup) chopped mixed fresh herbs such as rosemary, oregano, fennel and basil
450 ml (16 fl oz/2 cups) white wine or cider vinegar

In a wide-necked jar that herbs half-fill, place herbs and vinegar. Cover with a vinegar-proof lid. Leave in a warm place for 2 weeks; shake the jar daily.

Strain vinegar through cheesecloth. In a clean bottle place a spring of herbs. Pour in the vinegar. Seal with a vinegar-proof lid.

Variation:
English Herb Vinegar: Use 4 tablespoons chopped fresh sage and 6 tablespoons chopped fresh thyme in place of mixed herbs. Place a sprig of sage and a sprig of thyme in the bottle with the strained vinegar.

Tarragon Vinegar: Use 10 tablespoons chopped tarragon in place of mixed herbs. Place a sprig of tarragon in the bottle with stained vinegar.

FLAVOURED OILS

CHILLI OIL

6 small or 3 large fresh chillies
450 ml (16 fl oz/2 cups) second-grade olive oil, peanut oil or corn oil

GARLIC OIL

5 garlic cloves
1 teaspoon black pepper
450 ml (16 fl oz/2 cups) second-grade olive-oil, peanut oil or corn oil

If making chilli oil, prick chillies with a fork or point of a small, sharp knife. Slice large chillies. If making garlic oil, peel garlic cloves.

For chilli oil, place chillies in a clean bottle. Pour in oil. Seal. Allow to mellow 10 days. Will keep up to 2 months.

For garlic oil, place garlic, black pepper and oil in a clean bottle. Seal. Allow to mellow 10 days. Will keep up to 2 weeks.

HERB BUTTERS

BASIL BUTTER

125 g (4 oz/½ cup) butter, softened
8 to 10 fresh basil leaves, finely chopped

Beat butter and basil together until creamy. Press into a butter mould or roll into a cylinder and cover with cling film. Chill until firm.

MIXED HERB BUTTER

125 g (4 oz/½ cup) butter, softened
1 teaspoon each of finely chopped fresh parsley, sage, oregano and rosemary

Beat butter until creamy. Add the herbs and beat again. Roll into cylinders and cover with cling film, greaseproof paper or waxed paper. Refrigerate until firm.

GARLIC BUTTER

125 g (4 oz/½ cup) butter
4 cloves garlic, crushed
½ teaspoon white pepper
2 tablespoons finely chopped fresh parsley

Beat butter, garlic, pepper and parsley together until creamy. Press into a butter mould. Refrigerate until firm.

PICKLED GHERKINS

Fresh grape leaves, washed
1 kg (2 lb) small pickling cucumbers, washed and trimmed
30 g (1 oz/¼ cup) salt
3 l (88 fl oz/2 quarts) warm water
3 l (88 fl oz/2 quarts) white vinegar
105 g (3½ oz/½ cup) sugar
2 tablespoons whole peppercorns
2 cm (¾-in) piece fresh gingerroot
1 tablespoon whole allspice
1 tablespoon whole cloves
3 cloves garlic
1 tablespoon white mustard seeds
2 teaspoons grated nutmeg

Line a large glass or ceramic bowl with grape leaves. Place cucumbers in bowl. Dissolve salt in warm water. Cool. Pour brine mixture over cucumbers. Cover with grape leaves and let stand in a cool place for about 5 days, or until cucumbers become yellow.

Combine remaining ingredients and boil 5 minutes. Strain.

Wash cucumbers and pack tightly into sterilized jars. Pour pickling vinegar over cucumbers. Seal and leave in a warm place until cucumbers turn green again. Pour vinegar into a saucepan and bring to a boil. Allow to boil 3 minutes. Pour vinegar back into jars to cover cucumbers to within ½-cm (¼-in) of top. Seal with sterilized vinegar-proof lids. Store in a cool dark place – allow to mellow at least 2 weeks before using.

Makes 1.8 kg (4 lb./8 cups).

PICKLED WATERMELON

1 kg (2 lb.) watermelon rind, cut into pieces to fit jars
  (leaving some pink on rind)
125 g (4 oz/¾) cup salt
1.9 l (3¼ pts/2 quarts) water
1 kg (2 lb./5 cups) sugar
600 ml (1 pt/2½ cups) cider vinegar
1 lemon, sliced
1 cinnamon stick
1 teaspoon whole black peppercorns
1 teaspoon whole allspice
1 teaspoon whole cloves

In a glass or ceramic bowl, place rind, salt and water, cover; let stand overnight.

Drain and rinse rind. Place in a large saucepan, cover with water, bring to a boil. Simmer until rind is just tender, about 3 minutes.

Bring remaining ingredients to a boil and simmer 15 minutes. Strain liquid. Add watermelon rind and simmer until rind becomes translucent. Pack rind tightly into sterilized jars. Pour syrup to within ½-cm (¼-in) of top. Seal with sterilized vinegar-proof lids. Store in cool, dark place. Allow to mellow at least 1 month before using.

Makes 3 kg (6⅔ lb./12 cups).

— PICKLED MIXED VEGETABLES —

1 teaspoon dried oregano
4 carrots
4 celery sticks
2 green peppers
1 each red and yellow peppers
125g (4 oz/³⁄₄ cup) olives
1l (35 fl oz/4¹⁄₄ cups) white vinegar
310ml (10 fl oz/1¹⁄₄ cups) olive oil
105g (3¹⁄₂ oz/¹⁄₂ cup) sugar
2 teaspoons salt
¹⁄₂ teaspoon pepper
1 teaspoon dry oregano

Cut cauliflower into florets. Peel carrots and cut into even-sized sticks. String celery, cut into sticks. Seed peppers and cut into strips.

In a large enamel saucepan, combine vegetables, olives, vinegar, oil, sugar, salt, pepper and oregano. Bring to the boil, stirring to dissolve sugar. Cover and simmer 5 minutes. Uncover and let vegetables cool in the liquid.

Spoon the vegetables into sterilized jars. Bring liquid to boil and pour over vegetables to within ¹⁄₂-cm (¹⁄₄-in) of top of jars. Seal with sterilized vinegar-proof lids. Store in a cool, dark place – allow to mellow 2 months before using.

Makes 2.7kg (6lb./12 cups).

PICKLED ONIONS

1.5 kg (2½ lb.) small white boiling onions
125 g (4 oz/¾ cup) coarse salt
1.9 l (3¼ pts/2 quarts) white vinegar
45g (1½ oz/¼ cup) pickling spice, tied together in bag
made from several layers of muslin
450g (1lb./2¼ cups) sugar

Cover onions with boiling water. Let stand 2 minutes. Drain and dip in cold water. Peel. In a large ceramic bowl mix together onions and salt. Just cover with cold water. Cover and refrigerate. Boil vinegar, sugar and pickling spice bag for 5 minutes. Allow spices to cool in vinegar for 2 to 3 hours. Discard spice bag.

In sterilized jars to within ½-cm (¼-in) of top, pack onions firmly. Pour vinegar over onions and seal with vinegar-proof lids.

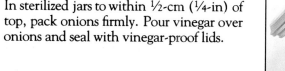

Store in a cool, dark place 3 months before using.

Makes 2.3kg (5lb./10 cups).

PICKLED MUSHROOMS

1 kg (2 lb.) small fresh mushrooms, rinsed
600 ml (1 pt/2½ cups) white wine vinegar
1 small onion, finely chopped
2 bay leaves
1 tablespoon whole black peppercorns
1 tablespoon coriander seeds
3 cardamom seeds

Trim and discard mushroom stems. In a large saucepan bring remaining ingredients to the boil and simmer 10 minutes.

Strain liquid, return to saucepan and add mushrooms. Simmer 5 minutes, or until mushrooms are tender but not soft.

Pack mushrooms into sterilized jars. Pour pickling liquid to within ½-cm (¼-in) of top. Seal with sterilized vinegar-proof lids. Store in a cool, dark, place – allow to mellow 3 weeks before using.

Makes 1.8 kg (4 lb./8 cups).

PICCALILLI

½ large cauliflower
1 cucumber
250 g (½ lb.) cooking apples
6 tablespoons salt
1 l (1 quart) water
450 g (1 lb.) onions
2 fresh green and red chillies
3 cloves garlic
4-cm (1½-in) piece fresh ginger root
125 ml (4 fl oz/½ cup) vegetable oil
2 tablespoons each black peppercorns,
turmeric and dry mustard
3 tablespoons cornflour
3.75 l (6½ pt/4 quarts) white wine vinegar

Chop cauliflower; peel and chop the cucumber and apples into small pieces. In a large, non-corosive bowl, mix together salt and water. Add cauliflower, cucumber and apples. Cover and refrigerate overnight.

In a food processor chop onions, chillies, garlic, and ginger. In a large frying pan, fry onions in oil until soft. Add all ingrediénts, except last 2. Cook 5 minutes.

Mix cornflour and 125 ml (4 fl oz/½ cup) vinegar. Pour remaining vinegar into frying pan, stir in cornflour/vinegar mixture. Cook, stirring, until thickened. Drain soaking vegetables. Rinse. Add to sauce; simmer just 10 minutes. Pour into sterilized jars. Seal with sterilized vinegar-proof lids.
Store in cool, dark place – allow to mellow 2 to 3 months before using.

Makes about 2.7 kg (6 lb./12 cups).

MINT JELLY

2.7 kg (6 lb.) cooking apples, washed, quartered
Juice of 4 lemons
125 g (4 oz/2 cups loosely packed) fresh mint leaves
250 ml (8 fl oz/1 cup) white wine vinegar
Sugar, see recipe
Chopped fresh mint leaves
Green food colouring
Mint flavouring, if desired

In a large heavy-bottomed saucepan, combine apples, lemon juice, mint; just cover with water. Simmer until apples are very soft. Add vinegar, and simmer 5 minutes more.

Strain mixture through a jelly bag or double thickness of muslin; do not force mixture through. Measure fruit juice and add 220 g (7 oz/1 cup) sugar for every 250 ml (8 fl oz/1 cup) of juice.

In a clean pan, cook juice and sugar over a low heat until sugar dissolves, stirring. Increase heat, boil briskly 5 minutes, without stirring, until proper consistency is reached when sugar temperature reaches 221F. Or, test using spoon method, page 64. Stir in chopped mint and a little colouring and mint flavouring if desired. Pour to within ¼-cm (⅛-in) of top of sterilized jars; cover; seal tightly with sterilized lids. Store in a cool, dark place.

Makes 2.7kg (6 lb./12 cups).

SAGE AND APPLE JELLY

2.7kg (6 lb.) cooking apples, washed, quartered (do not peel or core)
Juice of 4 lemons
250 ml (8 fl oz/1 cup) white wine vinegar
Sugar, see recipe
125 g (4 oz/2 cups) loosely packed, chopped sage, washed and divided into sprigs

In a preserving pan or a large, heavy-bottomed saucepan, combine apples and lemon juice; add enough water to cover fruit. Simmer until the apples are soft. Add vinegar and bring to a boil, boil 5 minutes.

Strain mixture through a jelly bag or double thickness of muslin for an hour. Do not press any apples through bag as this will cause jelly to cloud. Measure fruit mixture and add 220g (7 oz/1 cup) of sugar for every cup of juice. Pour back into preserving pan, bring to boil, stirring until sugar dissolves. Boil until temperature reaches 105C (221F). Or, test using spoon method, page 64.

Add sprigs of sage to sterilized jars. Pour jelly to within ¼-cm (⅛-in) of top of jars, cover; seal tightly with sterilized lids. Store in a cool, dark place.

Makes 2.7 kg (6 lb./12 cups).

PEACH CHUTNEY

1 kg (2¼ lb) peaches, peeled, stoned and chopped
450 g (1 lb./2 cups) chopped onions
310 ml (10 fl oz/ 1¼ cups) red wine vinegar
90 g (3 oz/½ cup) stoned dates, chopped
90 g (3 oz/½ cup) raisins
1 teaspoon salt
½ teaspoon ground ginger
½ teaspoon ground cinnamon
¼ teaspoon ground cloves
1 tablespoon mustard seeds
Grated peel and juice of 1 lemon
1½ cups packed brown sugar

In a large saucepan combine peaches with remaining ingredients, except sugar. Bring to a boil over high heat, stirring occasionally. Reduce heat and simmer peaches and onions until tender, stirring occasionally.

Add sugar and stir until dissolved. Simmer 2 to 3 hours, stirring frequently to prevent scorching, or until chutney is a rich brown colour and thick.

Fill sterilized jars with chutney to within ½-cm (¼-in) of top. Seal with sterilized vinegar-proof lids. Store in a cool, dark place – allow to mellow 6 weeks before using.

Makes about 1.5 kg (3 lb./6 cups).

SPICY APPLE CHUTNEY

1 kg (2 lb.) cooking apples
2 tablespoons salt
1 whole head garlic
2.5-cm (1-in) piece fresh ginger root
4 fresh green chillies, chopped
155 ml (5 fl oz/²⁄₃ cup) vegetable oil
2 tablespoons white mustard seeds
1 teaspoon each fenugreek, chilli powder and turmeric
15 whole black peppercorns
2 teaspoons ground cumin
155 ml (5 fl oz/²⁄₃ cup) vinegar
105 g (3½ g/½ cup) sugar

Peel, core and slice apples. In a large glass or ceramic bowl, place apples; and set aside. Peel and chop garlic and ginger, **chop chillies.**

In a large saucepan, gently fry garlic and ginger in oil for 3 minutes. Add spices and cook 5 minutes.

Add apples, vinegar and sugar; simmer until thick. Fill sterilized jars with chutney to within ½-cm (¼-in) of top. Seal with sterilized vinegar proof lids. Store in a cool, dark place.

Makes about 1.5 kg (3 lb./6 cups).

CHILLI NUTS

310 g (10 oz/2 cups) unblanched whole almonds or
peanuts
1 tablespoon chilli powder
1 large clove garlic, crushed
60 g (2 oz/¼ cup) butter, chopped
Coarse salt

In a heavy frying pan combine nuts,
chilli powder, garlic and butter.

Toss over medium heat until nuts
become crisp and lightly browned.

Sprinkle with salt and allow to cool.
Store in airtight containers.

Makes about 450 g (1 lb./2 cups).

SWEET SPICED NUTS

220 g (7 oz/1 cup) sugar
1 teaspoon salt
2 tablespoons ground cinnamon
1 teaspoon ground ginger
1 teaspoon ground cloves
½ teaspoon ground nutmeg
1 tablespoon water
1 egg white
155 g (5 oz/1 cup) whole nuts, such as peanuts,
cashews or almonds

Preheat oven to 120C (250F). Using a coarse sieve, sift sugar, salt and spices together 3 times. Beat together water and egg white. Dip nuts into egg white mixture.

Coat in sugar and spice mixture.

Spread nuts evenly on baking tray covered with greaseproof paper, making sure they don't touch. Bake 1½ to 2 hours. Remove from oven and allow to cool on baking tray. Shake excess sugar from nuts. Store in an airtight container.

Makes about 450 g (1 lb./2 cups).

MEXICAN PEANUTS

20 small dried red or green chillies, according to taste
4 cloves garlic, crushed
2 tablespoons olive oil
1 kg (2 lb.) blanched salted peanuts
1 teaspoon coarse salt
1 teaspoon chilli powder

In a heavy frying pan fry chillies and garlic in olive oil for a few minutes over low heat, stirring so chillies and garlic don't burn.

Add peanuts and continue frying and stirring until light brown.

Remove from heat and mix in salt and chilli powder. Cool. Store in airtight containers.

Makes about 1 kg (2 lb.).

MARINATED OLIVES

BLACK CARDAMOM OLIVES

450 g (1 lb.) large black olives in brine
1 orange
1 tablespoon cardamom seeds
Olive oil

Drain and rinse olives. Peel orange and cut skin (not white pith) into long strips. Place all ingredients into attractive jars and cover with olive oil. Cover, store in cool, dark place, – allow to mellow for at least 3 weeks before using.

GREEN CORIANDER OLIVES

450 g (1 lb.) large green olives in brine
8 to 10 cloves garlic
2 tablespoons coriander seeds, crushed
2 to 3 sprigs of fresh thyme

Drain and rinse olives, Place all ingredients into jars and cover with olive oil. Cover, store in cool, dark place – allow to mellow at least 3 weeks before using.

Each recipe makes about 450 g (1 lb.).

— GOAT CHEESE IN OLIVE OIL —

250 g (½ lb.) cylindrical goat cheese
4 large cloves garlic, peeled and sliced
3 or 4 sprigs of fresh rosemary and thyme
8 whole black peppercorns
Olive oil

Slice cheese into 8 equal rounds. Place in glass preserving jar with hinged lid.

Distribute garlic, herbs and peppercorns around cheese.

Cover with oil. Store in refrigerator – allow to mellow 24 hours before using. Will keep up to 2 weeks.

Makes 250 g (½ lb.).

SPIKED CHEESE BALLS

125 g (4 oz) blue cheese
125 g (4 oz) cream cheese
2 tablespoons vodka or calvados
2 tablespoons rye bread crumbs
60 g (2 oz/¼ cup) butter, softened
3 slices dark, rye bread, crusts removed
1 tablespoons caraway seeds
30 g (1 oz/¼ cup) almonds, toasted, finely ground

In a food processor or blender combine blue cheese, cream cheese and butter.

In a small bowl, mix vodka or calvados with breadcrumbs; let stand for 5 minutes. Blend breadcrumbs with butter and cheese mixture; chill 30 minutes, or until firm enough to handle.

In a food processor or blender, blend rye bread and caraway seeds into fine crumbs. Roll about 2 teaspoons of cheese mixture into balls; roll half of the balls in rye bread and half in almonds. Refrigerate until firm. Store in the refrigerator up to 1 week.

Each recipe makes about 30.

OLIVE CHEESE BALLS

125 g (4 oz/½ cup) grated mature Cheddar cheese, room temperature
3 tablespoons butter, softened
½ cup plain flour
½ teaspoon cayenne pepper
25 to 30 medium-sized stoned or stuffed olives

Preheat oven to 200C (400F). In a bowl cream together cheese and butter. Sift flour with pepper.

Add flour mixture to creamed mixture. Knead mixture with hands until fairly smooth.

Cover each olive with a teaspoon of dough. Place on lightly greased baking sheet. Bake 15 minutes, or until light golden brown. Cool on wire racks.
Store in an airtight container in a cool place. Will keep for up to 1 week.

Makes 25 to 30.

CHEESE AND WALNUTS

125 g (4 oz/½ cup) butter, room temperature
375 g (12 oz) Cheddar cheese, grated
6 tablespoons beer
½ teaspoon Dijon mustard
1 teaspoon Worcestershire sauce
½ teaspoon white pepper
105 g (3½ oz/⅔ cup) walnut halves

In a bowl beat butter until light and fluffy.

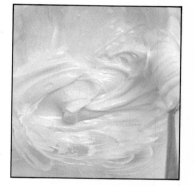

Add cheese and beer alternately; beat until well combined. Stir in remaining ingredients, except walnuts. Line a small container or ramekin with cling film.

Place half walnuts on bottom of container. Spoon half the cheese over walnuts. Cover with remaining walnuts; then remaining cheese. Smooth top. Refrigerate 24 hours. Turn out, upside down onto serving plate. Cover. Store in the refrigerator. Will keep up to 10 days.

Makes about 750 g (1½ lb.).

— STUFFED CHERRY TOMATOES —

450 g (1 lb.) cherry tomatoes, rinsed, patted dry
125 g (4 oz/³⁄₄ cup) ricotta cheese
8 fresh basil leaves, finely chopped
90 g (3 oz) soft blue cheese
60 g (2 oz/¹⁄₄ cup) cottage cheese, sieved
2 tablespoons fresh chopped chives
Ground black pepper
Celery leaves and chive sprigs, for garnish

With a sharp knife, cut cap off tomatoes. With a small spoon, remove seeds and turn tomatoes upside down onto paper towels to drain.

Beat ricotta cheese until smooth. Stir in basil and add pepper. Blend blue cheese with cottage cheese and chives until smooth. Add pepper.

With a small spoon, pack half the tomatoes with ricotta mixture and half with blue cheese mixture. Cover with caps, garnish with celery leaves and chive sprigs. Chill.

Makes 12 to 16.

PEARS STUFFED WITH GORGONZOLA

8 small ripe pears, peeled
Juice of 2 lemons, in a large bowl
125 g (4 oz) Gorgonzola cheese, softened
60 g (2 oz/¼ cup) butter, softened
30 g (1 oz/¼ cup), finely chopped walnuts or
pistachio nuts

Slice pears in half, taking care to leave
stem intact on one half. Core pears and,
with a spoon, remove a tablespoon of
the flesh to form a hollow. Immediately
immerse pears in bowl with lemon juice
to prevent discolouration.

In a small bowl, beat together cheese
and butter until smooth. Fill each pear
half with about a tablespoon of mixture.

Press pears together and roll in walnuts.
Refrigerate at least 2 hours. Serve as first
course. Store in the refrigerator up to 3
days.

Makes 8 servings.

BRIDGE CANAPÉS

Slices of white and brown bread, crusts removed
Cream cheese, softened
Red and black fish eggs
Thin slices of salami
Black olives, sliced or whole
Hard boiled eggs, sliced
Thin slices ham
Thin strips of red pepper, to garnish

Preheat oven to 100C (200F). Using biscuit cutters in shapes such as spades, hearts, diamonds and clubs, cut shapes from bread and bake until dry. Cool on a wire rack.

Cover canapés with cream cheese.

Garnish with red and black fish eggs, thin slices of salami, black olives, hard-boiled eggs, thin slices of ham and strips of red pepper. Use different garnishes for each shape of canapé.

FRITTATA

2 tablespoons olive oil
4 large onions, thinly sliced
2 cloves garlic, crushed
8 medium-sized courgettes, finely sliced
1 red chilli, finely chopped, if desired
Salt and pepper
8 eggs

In a large non-stick frying pan heat oil. Fry onions until soft. Add garlic and cook one minute more. Add courgettes and cook until just soft. Stir in chilli.

Beat eggs with salt and pepper. Pour over vegetables; stir gently.

Cook mixture until base is firm but eggs are still somewhat soft. Place pan under grill and brown top. Turn onto a platter and serve warm or cold. Store in refrigerator up to 3 days.

Makes 1 frittata.

BLUE CHEESE DIP AND CRACKERS

BLUE CHEESE DIP

155 g (5 oz/1 ½ cups) blue cheese, chopped
250 g (8 oz/1 cup) can crushed pineapple, drained
125 ml (4 fl oz/½ cup) sour cream
125 ml (4 fl oz/½ cup) cottage cheese
2 tablespoons fresh chopped chives
Chive sprigs, finely chopped chives, radish slices for
   decoration

In food processor or blender, blend all
ingredients, except chive sprigs.

When just combined, put into bowl or
bowls. Cover.

Decorate with chive sprigs, finely
chopped chives and radish slices. Store
in the refrigerator for up to 1 week.

Makes about 600 g (1¼ lb./2½ cups).

CHEDDAR CHEESE CRACKERS

125 g (4 oz/²⁄₃ cup) wholemeal flour
2 tablespoons self-raising flour
½ teaspoon salt
¼ teaspoon cayenne pepper
125 g (4 oz/½ cup) cup butter
60 g (2 oz/½ cup) grated Cheddar cheese
1 tablespoon lemon juice
1 egg

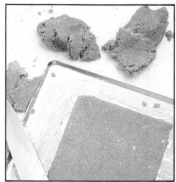

Preheat oven 160C (325F). In food processor or blender, combine all ingredients. Blend until dough is formed. Shape mixture into a roll 38-cm (15-in) long. Wrap in cling film. Refrigerate at least 3 hours. Cut roll into slices ½-cm (¼ in) thick, place on lightly greased baking sheets. Bake 15 minutes, or until light golden brown. Cool on baking sheets.
Makes about 60.

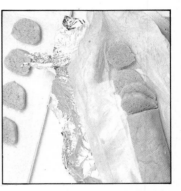

BRAN CRACKERS

60 g (2 oz/½ cup) unprocessed bran (available in hot cereal or flour section of supermarket)
125 g (4 oz/1 cup) wholewheat flour
1 tablespoon packed brown sugar
125 g (4 oz/½ cup) butter
2 eggs
Pinch of salt

Pre-heat oven to 160C (325F). In a food processor or blender, blend bran, flour, sugar and butter. Add eggs and salt. Blend until dough forms. Knead lightly on floured board; press into two 28×18-cm (11×7 in) tins. Prick surface with a fork. Bake 15 minutes or until light brown. Cut into squares; cool on a wire rack.
Makes about 35.

PEARL BALLS WITH DIPPING SAUCE

250 g (8 oz/1 1/4 cups) white long grain rice
4 dried Chinese mushrooms, or 6 fresh shiitake
   mushrooms
250 g (1/2 lb.) minced veal and minced pork
4 green onions, finely chopped
5 water chestnuts, sliced
1 teaspoon fresh grated ginger
1 clove garlic, crushed
2 tablespoons soy sauce
1 egg, beaten
1 teaspoon salt

DIPPING SAUCE:

125 ml (4 fl oz/1/2 cup) soy sauce
1/2 teaspoon sesame oil
1 tablespoon chilli sauce

Soak rice in cold water 2 hours. Drain
and spread onto kitchen towels. Soak
dried Chinese mushrooms in hot water
for 30 minutes, squeeze out water; finely
chop. Do not soak fresh mushrooms.
Combine mushrooms and remaining
ingredients in a large bowl. Mix well.

Roll mixture into walnut-sized balls; roll
in rice, to coat completely. Steam over
boiling water 30 minutes, or until rice
has swollen and is completely cooked.

DIPPING SAUCE:
In a small bowl, combine all
ingredients.

Makes about 30.

CHINESE CHICKEN WINGS

1 kg (2 lb.) chicken wings
2 tablespoons peanut oil
2 teaspoons sesame oil
125 ml (4 fl oz/½ cup) soy sauce
2 tablespoons honey
2 cloves garlic, crushed
1 teaspoon freshly grated ginger
½ teaspoon five spice powder
2 tablespoons dry sherry, if desired

Cut tips off chicken wings and discard. Place wings in a large bowl.

In a bowl mix remaining ingredients. Pour over chicken wings; stir to coat wings well. Cover and refrigerate 4 hours, or overnight.

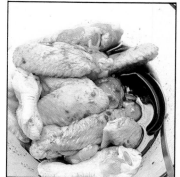

Preheat oven to 180C (350F). Place wings on lightly greased baking tray. Bake wings 30 minutes; turn and continue baking until they are golden brown, about 10 minutes. Drain on paper towels. Store in refrigerator up to 7 days.

Makes about 24.

SEAFOOD DIP

12 scallops
250 g (8 oz) cream cheese, cut into chunks
60 ml (2 fl oz/¼ cup) Mayonnaise, page 10
3 spring onions, chopped (use white part only)
1 small gherkin, finely chopped
2 teaspoons finely chopped fresh coriander or parsley
½ teaspoon chilli sauce
salt and pepper
20 prawns, shelled, deveined, cooked

Poach scallops until they are just opaque, being careful not to overcook. In a food processor or blender, place cream cheese, Mayonnaise, 6 scallops, spring onion, gherkin, coriander and chilli sauce; blend. Add salt and pepper and adjust other seasonings if necessary.

Chop remaining scallops and half the prawns. Combine scallops and all but a few prawns with cream cheese mixture.

Spoon into decorative serving containers. Decorate with remaining prawns. Store in the refrigerator up to 2 days.

Makes about 600 ml (1 pt/2½ cups).

POTTED SALMON

250 g (8 oz) smoked salmon
250 g (8 oz/1 cup) clarified butter
½ teaspoon ground white pepper
Pinch of salt
Sprigs of herbs, to decorate

In a food processor or blender, mix salmon, 185 g (6 oz/¾ cup) clarified butter and pepper.

Blend or process to a fine paste. Add salt to taste; refrigerate until firm. Press into a terrine or small attractive dishes.

Decorate with sprigs of herbs. Melt remaining 60 g (2 oz/¼ cup) clarified butter, let cool slightly, spoon over potted salmon, making sure it covers completely. Store in refrigerator up to 1 week.

Makes about 450 g (1 lb.)

FISH PÂTÉ

850 ml (1½ pt/1 quart) water
60 ml (2 fl oz/¼ cup) dry vermouth
1 small carrot, chopped
1 small onion, chopped
1 stalk celery, chopped
1 teaspoon black peppercorns
1 teaspoon salt
Sprig of parsley
Small piece of fresh fennel and thyme
1 bay leaf
250 g (½ lb.) fish fillets
2 teaspoons gelatine
2 tablespoons pimento, chopped
Salt and pepper
1 spring onion, finely chopped
Salt and pepper
Radishes, cucumber, lemon slices and red and black
fish eggs.

In a saucepan combine first 10 ingredients. Bring to boil; reduce heat and
simmer 30 minutes. Add fish; poach 10
minutes until flesh flakes when tested
with a fork.

Remove fillets; flake; cool. Reduce
liquid to 375 ml (12 fl oz/1½ cups).
Cool. When just warm, sprinkle gelatine on surface, stir to dissolve. In a food
processor, purée fish, pimentos, spring
onion, salt and pepper to texture that you
prefer, gradually adding fish stock.

Pour into a 550 g (1¼ lb./3-cup) mould;
refrigerate until set. Garnish with
radishes, cucumber, lemon slices and
red and black fish eggs. Store in the
refrigerator up to 3 days.

Makes about 1 kg (2 lb.)

CHICKEN LIVER PÂTÉ

250 g (½ lb.) onion, finely chopped
250 g (½ lb./1 cup) unsalted butter
2 cloves garlic, finely chopped
450 g (1 lb.) chicken livers, cleaned, fibrous membrane removed
2 hard-boiled eggs
2 tablespoons brandy
¼ teaspoon ground cloves
½ teaspoon ground allspice
½ teaspoon white pepper
½ teaspoon salt

In a large, heavy-bottomed frying pan, gently cook onions in butter until soft. Add garlic and chicken livers and cook until the livers are nicely browned on outside, but still pink on inside.

In a food processor or blender, combine contents of frying pan with remaining ingredients. Blend until the desired texture is achieved. It may be necessary to do this in batches.

Pack into ungreased 23 x 13-cm (9 x 5-in) loaf tin, terrine or pâté mould. Press firmly to make sure mixture fills corners. Cover tightly and refrigerate. Top may be weighted with brick if firmer pâté is desired. Store, well wrapped, in the refrigerator. Will keep up to 7 days.

Makes about 1 kg (2 lb.)

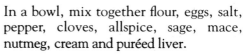

GRAND MARNIER PÂTÉ

675 g (1½ lb.) pork livers, cleaned, fibrous membrane removed
250 g (½ lb.) bacon, cut into pieces
125 g (4 oz/½ cup) butter, cut into pieces
1 medium-size onion, finely chopped
60 ml (2 fl oz/¼ cup) Grand Marnier (or other orange liqueur)
2 teaspoons grated orange peel
2 tablespoons plain flour
2 eggs, beaten
2 teaspoons salt
1 teaspoon white pepper
½ teaspoon ground cloves
½ teaspoon ground allspice
½ teaspoon ground sage
¼ teaspoon each ground mace and ground nutmeg
3 tablespoons whipping cream

ORANGE GLAZE:

375 ml (12 fl oz/1½ cups) clear chicken stock
1½ teaspoons gelatine
2 tablespoons Grand Marnier (or other orange liqueur)
Thin slices of orange, small sprigs of rosemary, celery leaves, black olives and strips of red pepper, to decorate

Preheat oven to 180C (350F). In a food processor or blender, mix livers, bacon, butter and onion until a smooth purée, add liqueur and orange peel. It may be necessary to do this in batches.

In a bowl, mix together flour, eggs, salt, pepper, cloves, allspice, sage, mace, nutmeg, cream and puréed liver.

Pack into an ungreased 23 x 13-cm (9 x 5-in) loaf tin, terrine on pâté mould. Put tin into a larger, deep baking tin. Fill larger baking tin with hot water to level of pâté mixture. Bake for 2½ to 3 hours. Remove pâté from larger baking tin and cool in baking tin.

ORANGE GLAZE:
Warm chicken stock, sprinkle gelatine over surface and stir to disolve slightly, add Grand Marnier. Decorate pâté with orange slices, small sprigs of rosemary, celery leaves, black olives and strips of red pepper.

Gently spoon the gelatine mixture over pâté a little at a time.

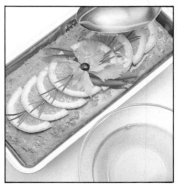

Store in the refrigerator – allow to set 24 hours before using. Will keep up to 3 weeks well-wrapped.

Makes about 1.5 kg (3 lb.)

PORK AND VEAL TERRINE

2 onions, finely chopped
2 cloves garlic, crushed
125 g (4 oz/½ cup) unsalted butter, chopped
250 g (½ lb.) each minced pork and veal
250 g (½ lb.) chicken livers, cleaned, fibrous membrane removed
250 g (½ lb.) pork livers, cleaned, fibrous membrane removed
125 g (4 oz/1 cup) good quality white bread pieces, crusts removed
185 ml (6 fl oz/½ cup) milk
60 ml (2 fl oz/¼ cup) dry vermouth
1 teaspoon dried thyme
½ teaspoon dried marjoram
½ teaspoon dried oregano
½ teaspoon dried sage
1 teaspoon salt
½ teaspoon black pepper
8 slices bacon
3 to 4 bay leaves

Preheat oven to 180C (350F). In a frying pan fry onions and garlic in butter over low heat until soft.

In food processor or blender, purée together cooked onions and garlic with minced pork and veal, and chicken and pork livers until smooth. It may be necessary to do this in batches.

In a large bowl, soak bread with milk and vermouth until soft. Add puréed mixture to bread and milk mixture. Stir in herbs and salt and pepper. Mix thoroughly.

Line a 23 x 13-cm (9 x 5-in) loaf tin, terrine or paté mould, with bacon allowing strips to hang over sides. Strips should be placed parallel to one another and crosswise in tin. Fill tin with meat mixture pressing it into sides and corners.

Cover top with a line of bay leaves and fold the bacon over top of mixture. Cover tightly with foil (and lid if using terrine). Put into a larger, deep baking tin. Fill larger baking tin with hot water to level of meat mixture. Bake 2½ to 3 hours. Remove tin from larger baking dish and place a weight, such as a brick, over the foil, pressing down on meat mixture.

Store in the refrigerator 12 hours. Remove weight. A further 12 hours or longer in the refrigerator will give the terrine a better flavour. Serve with Melba toast, or French bread. Store in the refrigerator up to 1 week.

Makes about 1.5 kg (3½ lb.)

RILLETTES

1.5 kg (3 lb.) pork belly
1 pigs foot, chopped in half
450 g (1 lb.) pork neck, cubed
450 g (1 lb.) back fat, cubed
2 cloves garlic, chopped
2 sprigs fresh thyme
1 bay leaf
1/4 teaspoon each ground cloves, nutmeg, ginger
1/2 teaspoon ground cinnamon
1 tablespoon salt
1 tablespoon white pepper
250 ml (8 fl oz/1 cup) white wine

Preheat oven to 150C (300F). In a large heavy casserole combine all ingredients. Cover with foil; cook 5 hours. Strain over a bowl. Set liquid aside.

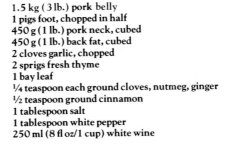

Remove meat from bones. Using two forks shred meat. Adjust seasoning and add a little of reserved liquid so texture is slightly creamy.

Pack meat firmly into a 23×13-cm (9×5-in) loaf tin or terrine mould. Carefully pour melted fat, which has been separated from reserved liquid, onto meat to a depth of 1.5-cm (1/2-in). Cover. Store in the refrigerator – allow to mellow 3 days before serving. Will keep up to 2 weeks.

Makes about 2–3 kg (5 lb.)

SPANAKOPITA

450 g (1 lb.) fresh spinach, trimmed
250 g (½ lb.) feta cheese
2 tablespoons finely chopped shallots
2 onions, thinly sliced
1 tablespoon finely chopped fresh thyme
1 tablespoon finely chopped rosemary
2 tablespoons finely chopped oregano
2 tablespoons finely chopped fennel
6 eggs
125 ml (4 fl oz/½ cup) vegetable oil
Salt and pepper
14 sheets filo pastry
185 g (6 oz/¾ cup) butter, melted

Preheat oven to 180C (350F). Steam
spinach leaves until limp. Cool, squeeze
out all moisture. Combine with cheese,
shallots, onion and herbs. In separate
bowl, beat together eggs, oil, salt and
pepper. Stir into spinach mixture.

Brush a 33 x 23-cm (13 x 9-in) baking
tin with a little of the melted butter. Lay
a sheet of filo in tin and brush lightly
with butter. Repeat using 6 more sheets.

Pour filling over filo layers. Top with
remaining filo sheets, brushing with
melted butter. Trim and tuck edges to
neaten. Bake 45 minutes, or until
golden brown. Cut into squares. Serve
warm or cold. Store in the refrigerator
up to 3 days.

Makes 1 pie.

ENGLISH PORK PIES

Stock:
850 ml (1½ pt/3½ cups) water
2 pigs trotters
1 large marrow bone
2 onions, chopped
Fresh bouquet garni
Pinch of salt
1 teaspoon ground white pepper

In a large saucepan, bring all ingredients to a boil. Lower heat, simmer 3 hours and allow to reduce to about 600 ml (1 pt/2½ cups). Strain, cool, skim off fat. Set stock aside.

Pastry:
250 g (8 oz) lard, chopped
250 g (8oz/2 cups) plain flour
Pinch of salt
2 teaspoons baking powder
boiling water

In a bowl, combine flour, salt and baking soda. Cut in shortening until mixture resembles coarse meal. Add sufficient boiling water to flour mixture to form into a stiff dough. Cover; leave to rest.

Preheat oven to 205C (400F). On a floured board, roll pastry to ¼-cm (⅛-in) thick. Cut eight 15-cm (6-in) circles and eight 8-cm (3-in) circles. Press 15-cm (6-in) circles into greased tins.

Filling:

1 kg. lean pork, diced
1 teaspoon salt
½ teaspoon ground white pepper
¼ teaspoon each ground mace, ground nutmeg and ground coriander
½ teaspoon ground thyme
2 fresh sage leaves, chopped
1 egg, beaten

In a bowl, combine, pork, salt, pepper, spices and herbs. Mix thoroughly and fill pastry-lined tins to within ½-cm (¼-in) of top. Brush edges of pastry with water. Top with 8-cm (3-in) circles; crimp edges to seal. Cut steam vents in tops. Brush tops with beaten egg.

Bake pies 20 minutes; lower oven temperature to 150C (300F) and bake 45 minutes. If pastry becomes too dark, cover loosely with foil. Remove pies from oven. Using a funnel, pour 2 to 3 tablespoons of prepared stock into each pie through hole in top.

Allow to cool, remove from tins. Store, covered, in cool place – allow to mellow 12 hours. Will keep up to 3 days.

Makes about 8 pies.

LEMON CURD

220 g (7 oz/1 cup) sugar
60 g (2 oz/¼ cup) butter, chopped
Grated peel of 2 lemons
Juice of 3 lemons
3 eggs, beaten

In a heatproof bowl or top of double saucepan placed over a saucepan of hot water, combine sugar, butter, lemon peel and lemon juice.

Place over a low heat; cook until butter melts, stirring occasionally.

Stir in eggs (do not let mixture boil, or it will curdle). Continue stirring over heat until mixture thickens. Pour into sterilized jars, seal with a sterilized lid, cool. Store in the refrigerator. Will keep up to 2 weeks. Use as a filling for flans or spread on bread and scones.

Makes 450 ml (16 fl oz/2 cups).

— HONEY AND APRICOT SPREAD —

12 dried apricots
375 g (12 oz/1 cup) set honey

In a bowl, place apricots and cover with boiling water; allow to stand at room temperature until softened.

Drain apricots. In blender or food processor, process apricots and honey.

When thoroughly combined, pour into a sterilized jar, seal with a sterilized lid; cool. Store in the refrigerator – allow to mellow 24 hours before using. You can easily double or triple this recipe.

Makes about 450 g (1 lb./2 cups).

APRICOT AND ALMOND CONSERVE

450 g (1 lb.) dried apricots, quartered
1.13 l (2 pts/5 cups) water
1.25 kg (2½ lb./6 cups) sugar
½ teaspoon almond liqueur or almond essence
60 g (2 oz/½ cup) blanched, slivered almonds

Soak apricots overnight in water. Strain apricots, reserve liquid.

In a heavy-bottomed saucepan combine reserved liquid and sugar, bring to boil over a low heat stirring until sugar is dissolved. Add apricots and simmer until temperature reached 105C (221F). Or, test using spoon method, page 64.

Immediately stir in liqueur and almonds. Remove from heat. Allow jam to stand at room temperature 10 minutes, stirring occasionally, to keep fruit and nuts in suspension. Pour conserve to within ¼-cm (⅛-in) of top of sterilized jars; seal tightly with sterilized lids. Store in a cool, dark place.

Makes 1.8 kg (4 lb./8 cups).

MINCEMEAT

250 g (8 oz/1¼ cups) raisins
250 g (8 oz/1¼ cups) currants
125 g (4 oz/½ cup) mixed candied peel
2 cooking apples, peeled
Grated peel of 1 lemon
Grated peel of 1 orange
125 g (4 oz/¾ cup) packed brown sugar
125 g (4 oz/½ cup) butter, melted
½ teaspoon each of ground nutmeg and ground
cinnamon
¼ teaspoon ground cloves
155 ml (5 fl oz/⅔ cup) brandy

Finely chop the raisins, currants and
mixed peel. Place in a bowl.

Chop apples and add with lemon and
orange peel, brown sugar, melted butter,
spices and brandy to raisin mixture.
Combine well. Cover and set aside in a
cool place for 3 days. Stir twice a
day.

Spoon into sterilized jars; cover; seal.
Store in the refrigerator – allow to mellow
2 weeks before using.

Makes about 1.6 kg (3½ lb./6 cups).

GRAPEFRUIT MARMALADE

2 kg (4 lb.) grapefruit, well scrubbed
Sugar, see recipe

Cut grapefruit into quarters, remove seeds and pithy centres. Put the seeds and centres in a 15-cm (6-in) square of muslin, tie into a bag. Peel grapefruit. Cut peel into julienne strips. Slice peeled fruit crosswise into thin slices. Separate slices into individual sections. Place fruit and bag in a large bowl; just cover with water. Soak 12 hours. Remove bag. In large preserving pan or saucepan, simmer fruit and soaking water 1 hour. For every cup of fruit and water add 155 g (5 oz/¾ cup) sugar. Bring to a boil; boil about 20 minutes or to proper consistency.

Test marmalade for doneness immediately after boiling. Proper consistency is reached when candy thermometer reaches 105C (221F). Or test by spoon test. Pour a small amount of marmalade onto a cold plate. Let stand until cold. If marmalade forms a skin and wrinkles when pushed with a finger or spoon, it is ready. Remove pan from heat while test preserve is cooling.

Cool 10 minutes; stir gently to mix skin through marmalade. Pour into sterilized jars to within 1-cm (½-in) of top. Seal with sterilized lids. Invert jars for a few seconds. Cool in upright position. Store in a cool, dark place.

Makes about 2.3 kg (5 lb./10 cups).

RUM AND PLUM JAM

1 kg (2 lb.) plums
2 lemons
1.25 kg (2½ lb./5¾ cups) sugar
2 tablespoons dark rum

Remove the stones and finely chop the plums; squeeze juice from lemons. In a large heavy-bottomed saucepan, combine fruit, sugar and lemon juice.

Bring to a boil over a low heat; stirring until sugar is dissolved. Increase the heat and boil 10 minutes, stirring to avoid burning until temperature reaches 105C (221F).

Or, test using spoon method, page 64. Remove pan from heat and stir in rum. Allow jam to stand 10 minutes, stirring at intervals so fruit doesn't sink. Pour to within ¼-cm (⅛-in) of top of sterilized jars; cover; seal tightly with sterilized lids. Store in a cool, dark place.

Makes about 1.8 kg (4 lb./8 cups).

MIXED CURRANT JELLY

1 kg (2 lb.) redcurrants, washed
1 kg (2 lb.) blackcurrants, washed
1.75 l (60 fl oz/7½ cups) water
Sugar, see recipe

In a preserving pan combine fruit and water. Bring to a boil and simmer until very soft.

Mash fruit with a wooden spoon and spoon into a jelly bag to drip overnight. Measure fruit juice and allow 220 g (7 oz/1 cup) sugar for each 250 ml (8 fl oz/1 cup) of juice.

Place sugar and liquid back in pan and bring to a boil, stirring to dissolve sugar. Boil 7 minutes until temperature reaches 105C (221F). Or, test using spoon method, page 64. Pour into sterilized jars; cover; seal tightly with sterilized lids. Store in a cool, dark place.

Makes about 3.6 kg (8 lb./16 cups).

— Microwave Strawberry Jam —

450 g (1 lb.) strawberries, washed, hulled, sliced
Juice of 1 lemon
345 g (11 oz/1½ cups) sugar
1 tablespoon butter

In a large bowl combine strawberries, lemon juice and sugar. Cook 20 minutes on high power, stirring occasionally.

Check for proper consistency by spoon method, page 64.

Stir butter into jam until dissolved. Allow jam to stand 30 minutes before bottling. Pour jam to within ¼-cm (⅛-in) of top of sterilized jars; cover; seal tightly with sterilized lids. Store in a cool, dark place.

Makes about 1 kg (2 lb./4 cups).

— ROSEMARY AND QUINCE JELLY —

3 kg (6 lb.) quinces
Juice of 3 lemons
Sugar, see recipe
3 tablespoons finely chopped rosemary

Wash and coarsely chop quinces; combine quinces and lemon juice in preserving pan or large, heavy-bottomed saucepan. Cover with water. Simmer uncovered until quinces are very soft. Strain mixture through a jelly bag or double thickness of muslin, being careful not to force mixture through, as this will cloud jelly.

Measure fruit juice and add 220 g (7 oz/1 cup) of sugar for every 250 ml (8 floz/1 cup) of juice. Return to pan, bring to a rolling boil. Boil briskly for 5 minutes until temperature reaches 105C (221F), or, test using spoon method, page 64.

Add finely chopped rosemary. Pour jelly to within ¼-cm (⅛-in) of top of sterilized jars; cover; seal tightly with sterilized lids. Store in cool, dark place.

Makes 3 kg (6 lb./12 cups).

FIGS IN BRANDY

14 dried whole figs
105 g (3½ oz/½ cup) sugar
1 cinnamon stick
Approximately 250 ml (8 fl oz/1 cup) brandy

In a large saucepan or frying pan, place figs in one layer with sugar and cinnamon stick. Just cover with water, poach over low heat 5 minutes. Discard cinnamon stick. Drain figs.

Pack figs in sterilized jar. Reduce syrup to half by simmering uncovered.

Half fill jar of figs with brandy. Pour reduced syrup in jar to within 1.5-cm (½-in) of top, cover. Store in a cool, dark place – allow to mellow at least 1 month before using.

Makes 750 g (1½ lb./3 cups).

BRANDIED PEACHES

440 g (14 oz/2 cups) sugar
250 ml (8 fl oz/1 cup) water
1 kg (2 lb.) peaches, halved, stoned and skinned (treat
with lemon juice to prevent discolouration, if desired)
Pinch of ground nutmeg
Approximately 250 ml (8 fl oz/1 cup) brandy

Combine sugar and water in large
saucepan. Heat to dissolve sugar. Add
fruit and nutmeg to syrup and simmer
until the fruit is just tender. Drain fruit
and pack into sterilized jars.

Bring syrup to a rolling boil and reduce
by half.

Half fill jars with brandy. Pour syrup
into jars to within 1.5-cm (½-in) of top.
If syrup runs short fill jars with more
brandy. Seal. Store in a cool, dark place
– allow to mellow 1 month before using.

Makes 1 kg (2 lb./4 cups).

PRUNES IN RUM

450 g (1 lb.) prunes
105 g (3 ½ oz/½ cup) sugar
250 ml (8 l oz/1 cup) water
Cinnamon stick
Rind of 1 lemon, cut into strips
Approximately 250 ml (8 fl oz/1 cup) dark rum

In a saucepan gently combine prunes, sugar, water, cinnamon stick, and lemon peel. Poach 5 minutes. Slit prunes lengthwise; remove stones. Pack prunes into a sterilized jar.

Boil syrup until reduced to 90 ml (3 fl oz/⅓ cup). Remove peel and cinnamon stick. Cool. Half fill jar with rum.

Top with syrup, adding more rum to cover prunes if necessary. Cover tightly. Store in a cool place – allow to mellow for 3 weeks. Will keep up to 3 months.

Makes about 750 g (1 ½ lb./3 cups).

MACEDOINE OF FRUIT IN BRANDY

450 g (1 lb.) mixed berries such as strawberries, raspberries, blueberries and gooseberries, rinsed
1 kg (2 lb.) sugar
Approximately 450 ml (16 fl oz/2 cups) brandy
450 g (1 lb.) mixed peeled, peaches, plums, nectarines and apricots, halved

In a sterilized preserving jar, layer berries with some of the sugar.

Pour brandy over to cover.

Layer peaches, plums, nectarines and apricots halves with remaining sugar over berries. Pour brandy over to cover. Continue layering to 1-cm (½-in) from top of jar. Seal. Store in cool, dark place – allow to mellow at least 2 months before using.

RUM BUTTER

2 egg yolks
1 tablespoon sugar
2 tablespoons rum
½ teaspoon vanilla essence
125 g (4 oz/½ cup) butter, softened

Combine yolks and sugar in a heatproof bowl or on top of a double saucepan; place over a saucepan of hot water. Beat yolks until they thicken and turn pale. Add rum and vanilla. Beat to combine.

Place a bowl or top of double saucepan into a large bowl of iced water. Beat egg mixture 1 minute to cool slightly. Beat in butter, a tablespoon at a time, until mixture is well combined.

Spoon into a container to firm. The mixture may be piped onto a plate when slightly softened if desired. Store the rosettes in one layer, covered, in the refrigerator. Will keep up to 1 week.

Makes about 185 g (6 oz/¾ cup).

— OLD FASHIONED GINGER BEER —

2 lemons
600 g (1¼ lb./3 cups) sugar
30 g (1oz) piece fresh ginger root, peeled and bruised
2 teaspoons cream of tartar
1 tablespoon brewers yeast
5 l (10 pt/5 quarts) boiling water

Carefully remove peel from lemons; remove and discard all white pith. Slice lemons thinly, removing seeds.

In a large glass or earthenware bowl, place lemon slices, peel, sugar, ginger and cream of tartar. Pour boiling water over mixture; let stand until tepid. Add brewers yeast and let stand in a warm place for at least 24 hours, or up to 2 days.

Skim the yeast from the top and strain liquid through muslin into sterilized bottles. Seal. Store in the refrigerator – allow to mellow 2 days before using.

Makes 5.5 l (10 pt/20 cups).

COFFEE LIQUEUR

450 ml (16 fl oz/2 cups) water
1 kg (2 lb/4½ cups) sugar
4 teaspoons instant coffee powder
Few drops vanilla flavouring
250 ml (8 fl oz/1 cup) brandy
250 ml (8 fl oz/1 cup) rum

In a saucepan combine water, sugar, instant coffee and vanilla. Heat gently, stirring until sugar and coffee have dissolved. Cool.

Stir brandy and rum into syrup.

Into a large decanter, pour coffee liqueur. Seal. Store in a cool, dark place – allow to mellow 2-3 weeks before using.

Makes about 1.8 l (3¼ pt/2 cups).

IRISH CREAM WHISKY

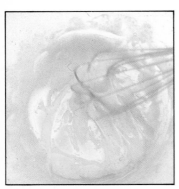

3 egg yolks
440 g (14 oz) can sweetened condensed milk
310 ml (10 fl oz/1¼ cups) whipping cream
375 ml (12 fl oz/1½ cups) whisky
1½ tablespoons sweetened chocolate syrup
¼ teaspoon coconut flavouring

In a large bowl, beat egg yolks until thick.

Stir in condensed milk, cream, whisky, chocolate syrup and coconut flavouring. Beat for 1 minute. Taste and add more coconut flavouring, if desired.

In a large decanter, pour Irish Cream Whisky. Seal. Store in refrigerator – allow to mellow 7 days before using. Will keep up to 2 weeks.

Makes about 1.15 l (2 pts/5 cups).

PEPPERMINT LIQUEUR

250 ml (8 fl oz/1 cup) water
440 g (14 oz/2 cups) sugar
1 teaspoon peppermint essence
375 ml (12 fl oz/1 ½ cups) brandy
½ teaspoon green food colouring

In a saucepan, combine water and sugar gently stirring. Heat until sugar dissolves. Cool.

Stir in peppermint essence, brandy and the food colouring. Pour into a sterilized decanter or bottle. If desired a few more drops of food colouring can be added. The syrup should be the colour of crème de menthe.

Seal and shake. Store in a cool, dark place – allow to mellow 7 days before using.

Makes about 800 ml (1 ½ pts/4 cups).

BLUEBERRY OR BLACKBERRY JELLIES

1 kg (2 lb.) fresh blueberries or blackberries, washed
440 g (14 oz/2 cups) sugar
2 tablespoons unsalted butter
375 ml (12 fl oz/1½ cups) liquid pectin
Caster sugar, for coating

Line a 25-cm (10-in) square cake tin with greaseproof paper. In a food processor or blender, place fruit and 220 g (7 oz/1 cup) sugar. Purée. It may be necessary to do this in batches. Pass fruit through a food mill, or force through a fine sieve into a large saucepan containing remaining 220 g (7 oz/1 cup) sugar.

Bring fruit to a boil over a low heat, stirring, boil 2 minutes more. Add butter and continue stirring and boiling 2 minutes more. Remove saucepan from heat. Stir in pectin. Pour into prepared tin and allow to set in cool place overnight.

Cut jelly into attractive shapes and roll in sugar. Store in a cool place in airtight containers with wax paper separating the layers. Will keep for up to 1 week.

Makes about 1 kg (2 lb.)

KIWI FRUIT JELLIES

1 kg (2 lb.) kiwi fruit, peeled and chopped
Juice of 1 lemon
750 g (1½ lb./3 cups) sugar
2 tablespoons unsalted butter
250 ml (8 fl oz/1 cup) liquid pectin
Green food colouring, if desired
Caster sugar, for coating

Line a 23-cm (9-in) cake tin with greaseproof paper. In a food processor or blender, combine fruit, lemon juice and 220 g (7 oz/1 cup) of sugar.

Purée. It may be necesary to do this in batches. Pass the liquid through a food mill or fine sieve into a large saucepan. Add remaining sugar; bring to boil, stirring constantly. Boil 3 minutes; add butter; still stirring, boil 3 minutes more. Remove from heat and stir in pectin and a few drops of colouring, if desired.

Pour into prepared tin and allow to set overnight in cool place. Cut into attractive shapes and roll in sugar. Store in a cool place in airtight containers with wax paper separating the layers. Will keep up to one week.

Makes about 1 kg (2 lb.)

SPICED DRIED FRUIT

220 g (7 oz/1 cup) sugar
1½ teaspoons grated lemon peel
1 teaspoon ground cinnamon
¼ teaspoon ground cloves
¼ teaspoon ground nutmeg
185 ml (6 fl oz/¾ cup) water
155 g (5 oz) dried apricots, pears, apples
Icing sugar

In a saucepan, combine sugar, lemon peel, spices and water. Cook over a low heat, stirring constantly, until sugar dissolves. Increase the heat, bring to a boil without stirring, boil to soft ball stage, 117C (240F) on sugar thermometer.

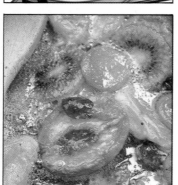

Add fruit and cook slowly 5 minutes, stirring to avoid burning. Remove saucepan from heat and immediately place it in a pan of warm water.

Using a fork, carefully lift out individual pieces of fruit, draining them over the pan. Roll fruit pieces immediately in icing sugar. Package in jars or decorative boxes.

Makes about 250 g (½ lb.)

APRICOT BALLS

90 g (3 oz/¹/₂ cup) dried apricots, chopped
90 g (3 oz/¹/₂ cup) stoned prunes, chopped
30 g (1 oz/¹/₄ cup) coarse raisins, chopped
3 tablespoons Cointreau or other orange liqueur
2 teaspoons grated orange peel
125 g (4 oz/1¹/₃ cups) desiccated coconut
90 g (3 oz/³/₄ cup) chopped walnuts
185 g (6 oz/³/₄ cup) sugar

In a bowl, combine apricots, prunes and raisins, sprinkle with Cointreau. Allow fruit to macerate at room temperature 1 hour, stirring occasionally.

In a food processor or blender, finely chop the fruit. In a bowl, combine chopped fruit, grated orange peel, 75 g (2¹/₂ oz/²/₃ cup) coconut and walnuts; mix thoroughly.

On a plate combine sugar and remaining coconut. Form fruit mixture into small, bite-size balls and roll in sugar and coconut mixture. Store in an airtight container with waxed paper between layers.

Makes 24 to 30 balls.

RUM BALLS

250 g (8 oz) plain biscuits
185 g (6 oz/1 cup) finely chopped mixed dried fruit,
such as raisins, apricots, prunes, figs or dates.
440 g (14 oz) can sweetened condensed milk
310 g (10½ oz/3 cups) unsweetened dessicated coconut
coconut
Grated peel of 1 lemon
2 tablespoons lemon juice
1 tablespoon cocoa powder
2 tablespoons dark rum

In a food processor or blender, finely crush the biscuits.

In a large bowl, combine biscuits, mixed dried fruit, condensed milk, 105 g (3½ oz/1 cup) of coconut, lemon peel and juice, cocoa and rum.

With wet hands, shape mixture into 3.25-cm (1¼-in) balls and roll in remaining 220 g (7 oz/2 cups) of coconut. Store in airtight containers in the refrigerator.

Makes about 45.

SUGARED ORANGE PEEL

5 oranges
600 g (1¼ lb./3 cups) sugar
3 tablespoons golden syrup
310 ml (10 fl oz/1¼ cup) water

Quarter oranges, remove pulp and scrape white pith from peel. Cut quarters (which are now just skins) into 1.5-cm (½-in) strips. In a saucepan, cover peel with water. Bring to boil. Simmer 10 minutes and drain. Repeat process twice more.

In a heavy-bottomed saucepan, bring 500 g (17 oz/2½ cups) sugar, syrup and water to a boil over a low heat, stirring until sugar is dissolved. Cook 20 minutes, without stirring, washing down any sugar crystals adhering to sides with a brush dipped in water. Add peel; continue simmering 15 minutes more, stirring to prevent sticking. Allow syrup to be almost completely absorbed by peel, making sure it doesn't burn.

Line 2 baking trays with greaseproof paper. Cover with remaining 100 g (3 oz/½ cup) sugar. Using a fork lift individual pieces of peel from pan and roll in sugar, coating peel well. Leave peel in single layer on baking trays overnight. Store in an airtight container, separating each layer with wax paper.

Makes about 250 g (½lb.)

Marzipan Fruits

125 g (4 oz/1¼ cups) finely ground almonds
125 g (4 oz/¾ cup) icing sugar (or more, if a sweeter flavour is desired)
1 egg white
Red, green, blue and yellow food colouring
A few cloves

In a heat proof bowl or top of a double saucepan placed over a saucepan of hot-water, place almonds; heat gently stirring occasionally until warmed. Remove double saucepan from heat, add sugar and egg white.

On a working surface, knead almond mixture until a smooth, fairly dry paste. Roll into a ball, cover with a cloth and let stand at room temperature for 15 minutes.

Break off small portions and shape into desired 'fruit'. The exact size of the fruit is up to you, but they should never be larger than a small walnut. You will need a couple of fine-pointed brushes, a saucer for mixing colours, a cup of water and a cloth for wiping brushes between colour changes. Remember, red and yellow make orange, diluted orange will put the base colour on peaches, red and green make brown for the stripes on bananas. Use cloves for the stem ends of oranges, pears and apples. You may make leaves from marzipan or use angelica.

Makes about 250 g (½ lb.)

CARAMELIZED FRUITS

140 g (4½ oz/⅔ cup) sugar
5 tablespoons water
Warm water
About 185 g (6 oz/2 cups) fresh assorted fruit, such as grapes, tangerine sections and strawberries, rinsed if necessary

In a heavy-bottomed saucepan, combine sugar and water. Cook over a gentle heat, cook, stirring occasionally, until sugar is dissolved.

Bring to a boil without stirring; boil until mixture turns a pale caramel colour. Remove immediately from heat; place in a bowl of warm water.

Carefully dip individual pieces of fruit into caramel. Place on a lightly greased baking sheet or wire rack; allow to cool and harden. To serve, place in petits fours cases. Fruit must be eaten within 24 hours. Do not refrigerate.

Makes about 750 g (1½ lb.)

CHOCOLATE DIPPED STRAWBERRIES

20 to 25 strawberries, washed and dried, leaves intact
185 g (6 oz) plain (dark) chocolate, chopped
2 teaspoons shortening

In top of a double saucepan, melt chocolate and shortening together over very low heat. Remove from heat.

Dip bottom half of each strawberry into chocolate mixture. Rest on greaseproof paper until set.

Place in paper sweet cases. Store, covered, in the refrigerator.

Makes 20 to 25 strawberries.

— CHOCOLATE COVERED PRUNES —

12 whole stoned prunes
12 whole Brazil nuts
250 g (8 oz) plain (dark) chocolate

Fill cavity of prunes with Brazil nuts.

In a heatproof bowl or the top of a double saucepan placed over a saucepan of hot water on a low heat, melt the chocolate, stirring.

Dip prunes into chocolate to coat completely. Place on greaseproof paper to set. Store, covered, in the refrigerator.

Makes 12 chocolates.

LEMON DROPS

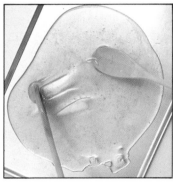

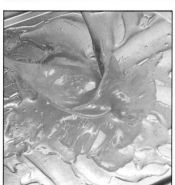

125 ml (4 fl oz/½ cup) water
300 g (9½ oz/1⅓ cups) sugar
¼ teaspoon cream of tartar
½ teaspoon lemon essence
1 teaspoon tartaric acid
Icing sugar

In a large heavy-bottomed saucepan, combine water and sugar, cook over medium heat, stirring to dissolve sugar. Bring to boil. Add cream of tartar and continue boiling until syrup reaches soft crack stage 140C (270F) on sugar thermometer. Remove immediately from heat – (make sure syrup doesn't burn – it should stay a pale yellow colour). Add lemon essence and tartaric acid. Pour syrup onto an oiled slab or a dish.

Using two wooden spoons, work into a toffee. Continue working until tofee becomes cool enough to handle with oiled hands. Pull toffee into a long roll.

With oiled scissors, cut off small pieces and shape with your hands into drops. Coat with icing sugar and allow the drops to cool and dry thoroughly. Store in airtight containers.

Makes about 250 g (½ lb.)

TOFFEE APPLES

450 g (1 lb./2¼ cups) sugar
125 g (4 oz/½ cup) butter
2 tablespoons white wine vinegar
2 tablespoons boiling water
Red food colouring, if desired
Hot water
8 medium-sized crisp apples, washed, dried, skewered
from top with 8 wooden lollipop sticks or skewers
Iced water

In a heavy-bottomed saucepan, combine sugar, butter, vinegar, boiling water and a few drops of red food colouring, if desired. Cook over low heat, stirring, until sugar is dissolved. Increase heat and boil, without stirring, until mixture reaches hard crack stage 147C (290F) on sugar thermometer or using a spoon, drop a little toffee into a small bowl of cold water to test.

Place saucepan in a larger saucepan of hot water to keep toffee soft. Quickly dip apples in toffee mixture, repeat for a thicker coating.

Dip coated apples into iced water to harden the toffee. Stand on greaseproof paper to cool. Wrap toffee apples in cling film.

Makes 8 toffee apples.

NUT TOFFEES

440 g (14 oz/2 cups) sugar
125 g (4 oz/½ cup) butter, chopped
2 tablespoons white vinegar
2 tablespoons boiling water
Assortment of unsalted nuts, such as pecans, almonds, walnuts and pistachio nuts

In a heavy-bottomed saucepan, combine sugar, butter, vinegar and boiling water. Place over a low heat and stir until sugar is dissolved. Increase the heat; cook without stirring until mixture changes colour. Start testing by spooning mixture by drops into a small bowl of ice water. When a firm ball is produced (test by feeling), toffee is done. Or cook to 147C (290F) on sugar thermometer.

Pour into a well-buttered 23-cm (9-in) square tin. Let cool.

Mark into pieces with a sharp knife, Place nuts in each square. Let cool completely and harden. Turn out onto a wooden board and break into pieces. Wrap in foil or cling film.

Makes about 450 g (1 lb.)

MIXED TOFFEES

900 g (2 lb./4½ cups) sugar
250 g (8oz/1 cup) butter
60 ml (2 fl oz/¼ cup) white vinegar
4 tablespoons boiling water
24 patty pans
Glacé cherries and nuts, to decorate

In a large heavy-bottomed saucepan, bring sugar, butter, vinegar and water to a boil.

Boil until the colour changes and then start testing by dropping the mixture by drops into a teacup or glass of iced water. When a firm ball is produced (test by feeling) or, cook to 147C (290F) on sugar thermometer. Spoon immediately into small candy moulds.

Decorate with cherries and nuts.

Makes about 24.

BUTTERED BRAZIL NUTS

60 g (2 oz/½ cup) whole Brazil nuts
90 ml (3fl oz/⅓ cup) water
200 g (6½ oz/1 cup) demerara sugar
1½ teaspoon liquid glucose
1¼ teaspoon cream of tartar
60 g (2 oz/¼ cup) butter, chopped

Preheat oven to 110C (225F). On an oiled baking sheet spread nuts in a single layer. Warm in the oven for 5-10 minutes while preparing the toffee mixture.

In a heavy-bottomed saucepan, combine water and sugar. Cook over low heat until sugar is dissolved. Bring liquid to boil, add glucose, cream of tartar and butter, simmer until butter has melted. Bring to a boil and boil until soft crack stage 140C (270F) is reached with sugar thermometer.

Remove saucepan from heat. Remove nuts from oven. With a spoon, drizzle a little toffee over each nut. Leave to cool and harden. If toffee is setting too quickly in the pan, place it in a bowl of hot water. Wrap individually. Store in a cool, dark place.

Makes about 450 g (½ lb.)

CHOCOLATE LOGS

60 g (2 oz/¼ cup) mixed candied peel, finely chopped
60 g (2 oz/¼ cup) raisins, coarsely chopped
60g (2 oz/½ cup) chopped almonds
2 tablespoons finely chopped preserved ginger
2 tablespoons chopped walnuts
1 tablespoon sugar
60 g (2 oz/⅔ cup) desicated coconut
410 g (13 oz) plain (dark) chocolate
125 ml (4 fl oz/½ cup) dark or light rum
Icing sugar

In a large bowl, combine candied peel, raisins, almonds, ginger, walnuts, sugar and coconut, set aside. Melt 155 g (5 oz) chocolate in top of double saucepan taking care not to let water boil, so chocolate doesn't get too warm.

Mix chocolate with dry ingredients; add the rum. Let cool slightly. On a surface lightly coated with icing sugar shape chocolate mixture into finger-sized logs. Refrigerate until firm.

Melt remaining chocolate; let cool slightly. Dip cold logs in warm chocolate, covering each one thoroughly. Place on greaseproof paper. With a fork draw lines over the warm chocolate, to resemble bark. Let set at room temperature. Wrap in cellophane or cling film. Box several logs together. Store in a cool place or the refrigerator.

Makes about 1 kg (2 lb.)

EASY CHOCOLATE FUDGE

125 g (4 oz/½ cup) butter
105 g (3½ oz/½ cup) sugar
2 tablespoons cocoa powder
2 tablespoons desiccated coconut
60 g (2 oz/½ cup) chopped walnuts
60 g (2 oz/⅓ cup) chopped glacé cherries
90 g (3 oz/½ cup) chopped crystallized ginger
1 tablespoon grated orange peel
½ teaspoon vanilla essence
250 g (8 oz) biscuits, crushed
1 egg, beaten

In a heavy-bottomed saucepan, combine butter, sugar and cocoa. Cook, stirring occasionally, over low heat until butter melts and sugar is dissolved.

Remove from heat and stir in coconut, walnuts, cherries, ginger, orange peel, biscuits and egg. Mix well and press mixture into an oiled 20 x 23-cm (8 x 9-in) cake tin.

Chocolate Icing:

155 g (5 oz/1 cup) icing sugar
2 tablespoons unsweetened cocoa powder
1 tablespoon butter, softened
2 tablespoons water

Sift icing sugar and cocoa into a bowl. Add butter and water. Beat until smooth. Spread icing over fudge. Cut into pieces. Store in an airtight container.

Makes about 450 g (1 lb.)

MOCHA NUT FUDGE

450 g (1 lb./2¼ cups) sugar
310 ml (10 fl oz/1¼ cups) whipping cream
310 g (10 fl oz/1¼ cups) butter, chopped
155 ml (5 fl oz/⅔ cup) strong black coffee
250 g (8 oz) bitter sweet chocolate, coarsely chopped
155 g (5 oz/1 cup) chopped Brazil nuts, hazelnuts or walnuts

In a heavy-bottomed saucepan over a low heat, combine sugar, cream, butter and coffee. Cook, stirring occasionally until sugar dissolves. Add chocolate to sugar mixture. Raise heat and bring to a boil stirring frequently.

Allow mixture to reach softball stage on your sugar thermometer 114C (234F). Stir in nuts.

Remove from heat and beat fudge until it begins to thicken. Immediately pour out into an oiled 20-cm (8-in) baking tin. Let fudge cool and cut into squares. Wrap individual pieces in cling film.

Makes about 1 kg (2 lb.)

CHOCOLATE TRUFFLES

60 g (2 oz/⅓ cup) sliced almonds
90 g (3 oz/⅓ cup) sugar
750 g (1½ lb.) plain (dark) chocolate, chopped
1 tablespoon strong coffee
75 g (2½ oz) butter, softened
2 tablespoons whipping cream
2 liqueurs of your choice
cocoa powder

In a small, heavy-bottomed pan, combine almonds and sugar. On a low heat, slowly cook to a pale golden brown, stirring with a wooden spoon until dark brown. Remove from heat immediately and pour onto an oiled plate. Allow to harden. In a food processor or blender, crush nut mixture to a coarse powder.

Melt 250 g (8 oz) chocolate in a bowl or top of a double saucepan set over a pan of simmering water. Stir in coffee; cool slightly. Beat in butter; stir in cream and crushed nut mixture. Divide mixture in half, flavour each half with 1 or 2 tablespoons of liqueur.

Gently roll heaping teaspoons of mixture into balls. Work quickly as chocolate sets fast. Set aside on greaseproof paper; refrigerate until firm. Melt remaining chocolate; dip some truffles and place on greaseproof paper to set. Roll others in cocoa when almost set. Place on greaseproof paper to dry, or place in sweet cases. Store, covered, in a cool place.

Makes about 1 kg (2 lb.)

— Chocolate Liqueur Shells —

90 g (3 oz) each of plain (dark), milk and white chocolate, melted separately

Mousse:
90 g (3 oz) white chocolate, chopped
2 eggs, separated
1 tablespoon each of Tia Maria, crème de menthe or Cointreau
Food colouring, if desired

With a spoon, smear chocolate evenly over inside of 12 paper sweet cases. Turn cases upside down on a plate. Refrigerate until set. Gently peel off the paper.

Mousse:
Slowly melt white chocolate. Remove from heat; quickly beat in egg yolks. In a separate bowl, beat egg whites until stiff, but not dry. Divide egg yolk mix into three separate bowls and add 1 teaspoon of a different liqueur to each. Add a little green food colouring to crème de menthe, a little yellow colouring to Cointreau. Gently fold a third of the egg whites into each of the bowls.

Divide between chocolate shells. Refrigerate 2 hours. Eat within 24 hours. The chocolate cases can be made in advance and stored in a cool, dry place.

Makes 12 sweets.

ICE CREAM EASTER EGGS

1 kg (2 lb.) plain (dark) chocolate, chopped
(quick alternative: carefully slice and half 4 purchased chocolate eggs)

Egg White Filling:
125 g (4 oz) white chocolate, chopped
60 ml (2 fl oz/¼ cup) whipping cream
2 eggs, room temperature
2 tablespoons sugar
½ teaspoon vanilla essence

Egg Yolk Filling:
310 ml (10 fl oz/1¼ cups) milk
1 egg yolk
1 tablespoon sugar
1 tablespoon custard powder
2 tablespoons chopped almonds
4 dried apricots, finely chopped
2 teaspoons brandy
Few drops yellow food colouring
125 g (4 oz) plain (dark) chocolate, chopped, for assembling eggs
Crystallized flowers for decoration

Egg Shells:
In the top of a double saucepan or heatproof bowl placed over a saucepan of hot water, place chocolate. Place pan over a moderate heat until chocolate melts, stirring occasionally. Spread a thin layer of chocolate inside moulds. Place moulds open side down on a flat surface and refrigerate until firm.

Egg White Filling:
Melt white chocolate and set aside to cool. Beat cream until soft peaks form, set aside. Beat eggs with sugar and vanilla until thick and creamy. Place egg mixture on top of double saucepan. Place over simmering water, cook, stirring until mixture thickens; cool to

room temperature. Stir in white chocolate until the mixture is smooth. Cool. Fold in whipped cream. Pour into trays. Freeze until almost completely frozen.

Egg Yolk Filling:
In a bowl, combine almonds, chopped apricots and brandy. Allow to stand at room temperature 30 minutes. Beat milk, yolk and sugar together. Stir in custard powder. Bring to a simmer and stir until thickened. Add a few drops of yellow food colouring. Combine custard mixture with apricot mixture. Cool. Place in freezer until almost completely frozen.

To assemble chocolate eggs, spoon semi-frozen 'egg-white filling' into each of the chocolate egg shells. Make an indentation with the back of a spoon in the centre of each egg (this is to make room for the 'yolk'.) Roll egg yolk filling into 4 balls and place in only four of the egg halves.

Melt 125 g (4 oz) chocolate. With a warm knife or skewer, run melted chocolate over edges of eggs. Gently press egg shells together, making sure you have one half with the yolk and the other hollow.

Freeze overnight. Decorate with piped names and candied flowers.

Makes 4 eggs.

HERB MUFFINS

250 g (8 oz/2 cups) plain flour, sifted
2 tablespoons sugar
1 tablespoon baking powder
Pinch of salt
1 egg
125 ml (4 fl oz/½ cup) milk
2 tablespoons butter, melted
60 g (2 oz/1 cup) lightly packed, fresh herbs (parsley, thyme, oregano, or sage), finely chopped

Preheat oven to 190C (375F). Sift flour, sugar, baking powder and salt together. Set aside. Beat egg and milk together, add melted butter.

Quickly stir liquid ingredients into flour. Stir until just moistened. Mix in herbs.

Pour into greased muffin pans. Bake 15 to 20 minutes or until fine skewer inserted in centre comes out clean. Turn out on to wire rack to cool.

Makes 12 muffins.

SULTANA BRAN MUFFINS

185 g (6 oz/1¼ cups) plain flour
1 teaspoon baking powder
1 teaspoon bicarbonate of soda
Pinch of salt
125 g (4 oz/2¼ cups) bran
185 g (6 oz/¾ cup) sugar
250 ml (8 fl oz/1 cup) milk
90 g (3 oz/½ cup) sultanas
1 tablespoon golden syrup
60 g (2 oz/¼ cup) butter

Preheat oven to 220C (425F). Sift flour, baking powder, bicarbonate of soda and salt together; add bran and sugar.

In a saucepan warm milk, sultanas, golden syrup and butter together until butter melts. Pour mixture into dry ingredients; stir until just moistened.

Spoon into greased muffin pans. Bake 12 to 15 minutes, or until fine skewer inserted into centre of muffin comes out clean. Turn onto a wire rack to cool.

Makes 12 muffins.

SCOTTISH SHORTBREAD

250 g (8 oz/1 cup) butter, softened
105 g (3½ oz/½ cup) caster sugar
60 g (2 oz/¼ cup) rice flour, sifted
280 g (9 oz/2⅔ cups) plain flour, sifted

Preheat oven to 150C (300F). Cream butter and sugar together.

Stir in flours; use your hands as mixture becomes too stiff to work with a spoon. On a lightly floured surface, knead mixture until smooth.

Gently press to desired thickness (this mixture does not roll). Cut into shapes, or use a shortbread mould (dusted with cornflour to make unmoulding easier). Or, take portions of dough and press into baking tins such as pie plates, or 20-cm (8-in) square baking tins. Bake about 1 hour or until just beginning to turn golden. Turn out onto a wire rack to cool. Store in an airtight container. The quantity of shortbread this recipe yields depends upon the thickness and size you choose to make the shortbread.

MUESLI BARS

125 g (4 oz/¹/₂ cup) butter, chopped
60 g (2 oz/¹/₄ cup) peanut butter
185 g (6 oz/¹/₂ cup) honey
155 g (5 oz/1 cup) packed brown sugar
185 g (6 oz/2 cups) rolled oats
125 g (4 oz/1 cup) puffed rice cereal
125 g (4 oz/1 cup) bran flakes
50 g (1¹/₄ oz/¹/₂ cup) bran
40 g (1¹/₄ oz/¹/₂ cup) wheatgerm
50 g (1¹/₄ oz/¹/₂ cup) desiccated coconut
20 g (³/₄ oz/¹/₄ cup) sesame seeds
75 g (2¹/₂ oz/¹/₂ cup) sunflower seeds
75 g (2¹/₂ oz/¹/₂ cup) pumpkin seeds
60 g (2 oz/¹/₂ cup) pine nuts
75 g (2¹/₂ oz/¹/₂ cup) dried apricots, chopped

Heat butter, peanut butter, honey and sugar in a large heavy frying pan until butter melts and sugar dissolves. Stir occasionally to blend.

Add remaining ingredients. Cook 10 minutes, or until golden brown, stirring to prevent burning.

Turn into 23 x 33-cm (9 x 13-in) greased baking tin. Press mixture lightly. Allow to cool. Cut into bars, and wrap in foil or cling film. Store in a cool place in an airtight container.

Makes about 35 bars.

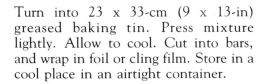

CHOCOLATE FINGERS

125 g (4 oz/1 cup) icing sugar
125 g (4 oz/1 cup) powdered milk
3 tablespoons cocoa powder
60 g (2 oz/⅓ cup) raisins
60 g (2 oz/⅓ cup) glacé cherries
60 g (2 oz/⅓ cup) mixed candied peel
vanilla extract
250 g (8 oz/1 cup) vegetable shortening, melted

Sift icing sugar, powdered milk and cocoa into a bowl. Add fruit and toss until fruit is well coated.

Stir in shortening and a few drops of vanilla. Mix thoroughly.

Pour mixture into a 20-cm (8-in) square baking tin lined with cling film. Refrigerate until firm. Turn out onto a board and cut into fingers. Wrap pieces in foil or cling film. Store in an airtight container in a cool place.

Makes about 32 fingers.

GINGER BISCUITS

125 g (4 oz/½ cup) butter, chopped
90 g (3 oz/¼ cup) golden syrup
105 g (3½ oz/½ cup) sugar
310 g (10 oz/2 cups) plain flour
1 tablespoon ground ginger
1 teaspoon bicarbonate of soda
250 g (8 oz/1¾ cups) icing sugar
Juice of 1 lemon, strained, warmed
1 teaspoon butter

Preheat oven to 190C (375F). In a bowl placed over a saucepan of hot water, place butter, golden syrup and sugar. Stir until butter is melted and sugar is dissolved. Remove from heat.

Sift flour, ginger and bicarbonate of soda. Stir into warmed mixture until a stiff dough is formed. Wrap in cling film; refrigerate 20 minutes.

Roll out on a floured board to 5-mm (⅛-in) thickness and cut into 5-cm (2-in) rounds. Place on greased baking sheet and bake 15 to 20 minutes, or until lightly browned. Cool on a wire rack.

Icing:
Sift icing sugar into a small bowl. Stir in lemon juice and butter until smooth. Spread icing onto cold biscuits.

Makes about 30 biscuits.

– RASPBERRY HAZELNUT BISCUITS –

125 g (4 oz/¹⁄₂ cup) butter
90 g (3 oz/¹⁄₃ cup) sugar
90 g (3 oz/³⁄₄ cup) ground hazelnuts
1 teaspoon lemon juice
1 teaspoon vanilla essence
185 g (6 oz/1¹⁄₄ cups) plain flour, sifted

Raspberry Glacé Icing:

250 g (8 oz/1³⁄₄ cups) icing sugar
1 teaspoon butter
1 to 2 teaspoons raspberry essence or raspberry liqueur
1¹⁄₂ tablespoons hot water

Preheat oven to 160C (325F). Cream together butter and sugar until light and fluffy.

Stir in hazelnuts, lemon juice and vanilla. Mix in flour to form a firm dough.

On a floured board, roll out to ¹⁄₄-cm (¹⁄₈-in) thickness and cut into 5-cm (2-in) rounds. Place on greased baking sheet and bake 10 to 15 minutes, or until lightly browned. Cool on wire rack.

Icing:
Sift icing sugar into a bowl; add butter **and raspberry essence or liqueur. Stir** in 1¹⁄₂ tablespoons hot water, drop by drop, until mixture is of spreading consistency. You may not need all the water. Spread icing onto completely cooled biscuits.

Makes about 30 biscuits.

WALNUT AND CHOCOLATE BISCUITS

155 g (5 oz/1¼ cup) plain flour
125 g (4 oz/½ cup) icing sugar
½ teaspoon ground cinnamon
125 g (4 oz/½ cup) butter, chopped
125 g (4 oz/1 cup) ground walnuts
1 teaspoon grated lemon peel
1 egg yolk, beaten

Chocolate Icing:
60 g (2 oz) plain (dark) chocolate
½ teaspoon margarine

Preheat oven to 160C (325F). Sift flour, icing sugar and cinnamon together into a bowl. Cut in butter until mixture resembles coarse meal. Stir in ground **walnuts, lemon peel and egg yolk.**

Turn mixture onto floured board and knead until smooth. Roll out on a **floured board ¼-cm (⅛-in) thickness** and cut into 5-cm (2-in) rounds. Place on a greased baking sheet and bake 10 to 15 minutes, or until lightly browned. Cool on a wire rack.

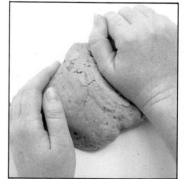

Icing:
In a double saucepan very slowly melt chocolate and margarine over warm water. Dip half of each biscuit into melted chocolate mixture. Refrigerate on waxed paper until chocolate is set.

Makes about 40 biscuits.

BRANDY SNAP BASKETS

60 g (2 oz/¼ cup) butter, chopped
60 g (2 oz/¼ cup) sugar
2 tablespoons golden syrup
60 g (2 oz/½ cup) plain flour
½ teaspoon ground ginger
1 teaspoon brandy or rum flavouring

Preheat oven to 180C (350F). Cut nine 15×15-cm (6×6-in) squares of greaseproof paper. In a saucepan combine butter, sugar and syrup, cook over a low heat until butter melts. Sift flour and ginger together. Stir into butter mixture. Add brandy flavouring and mix well.

Place greaseproof paper on baking sheets. Drop a tablespoon of mixture onto centre of each square. Bake 7 minutes, or until the biscuits are a dark golden brown.

Remove from oven and rest for a minute. Place biscuits over the base of inverted lightly greased glasses and gently peel off paper. Allow to cool.
To serve, fill with ice cream, whipped cream, and/or fresh fruit. Store, unfilled, in an air tight container.

Makes about 9.

FLORENTINES

60 g (2 oz/¼ cup) unsalted butter
60 g (2 oz/⅓ cup) packed brown sugar
2 tablespoons plain flour, sifted
30 g (1 oz/¼ cup) finely chopped walnuts
30 g (1 oz/¼ cup) sliced almonds
30 g (1 oz/¼ cup) finely chopped hazelnuts
1 tablespoon finely chopped glacé cherries
2 tablespoons, finely chopped mixed candied peel
125 g (4 oz) plain (dark) chocolate
1 teaspoon margarine

Preheat oven to 180C (350F). Cream butter and sugar together until fluffy. Mix in flour, stir in nuts, cherries and candied peel. Drop mixture by tablespoons onto greased baking sheets leaving 10 to 13-cm (4 to 5-in) between each biscuit (mixture spreads as it bakes).

Bake 4 minutes or until biscuits are golden brown. Allow to rest for 1 minute before removing onto a wire rack to firm and cool.

In a double saucepan, slowly melt chocolate with margarine. Spread chocolate over smooth underside of biscuit and, using a fork, score the chocolate in waves. Refrigerate until set. Store in an airtight container in a cool place.

Makes about 30.

CHOCOLATE BOXES

2 eggs, room temperature
30 g (1 oz/¼ cup) sugar
60 g (2 oz/½ cup) plain flour, sifted
2 tablespoons butter, melted
36 chocolate squares or orange flavoured chocolate squares about 6.5-cm (2½-in) square
Orange marmalade, warmed
12 to 18 caramelized tangarine segments, page 85
310 ml (10 fl oz/1¼ cups) whipping cream, lightly whipped

Preheat oven to 220C (425F). Beat eggs and sugar together until pale lemon in colour and thick. Fold flour alternately into egg mixture with melted butter. Pour into a greased and floured 20-cm (8-in) square cake tin. Bake 8 to 10 minutes or until toothpick inserted into centre comes out clean. Turning out on to a wire rack. Cool cake completely then cut into 2.5-cm (1-in) square pieces.

Lay 2 pieces of 45-cm (18-in) long ribbon in a cross on wax paper. Place a chocolate square over centre of ribbons; brush lightly with marmalade. Top with piece of cake, brush sides of sponge with marmalade. Press a chocolate square on all 4 sides of cake.

Spoon in whipped cream, top with 2 or 3 caramelized tangarine segments. Rest a square of chocolate, tilted slightly upward, on top as lid. Tie ribbons together in a bow. Repeat for all six boxes. Will keep up to 24 hours.

Makes 6

PETITS FOURS

125 g (4 oz/½ cup) almond paste
220 g (7 oz/1 cup) sugar
8 eggs
250 g (8 oz/1 cup) butter
1 teaspoon vanilla extract
375 g (12 oz/2½ cups) plain flour
1 tablespoon baking powder
450 g (1 lb.) fondant icing
Almond and vanilla essences
Green, pink and yellow food colourings
Almond slivers, walnut halves, candied violets, candied
    fruits, for decoration

Preheat oven to 350F (180C). In a bowl,
mix together marzipan with 105 g (3½
oz/½ cup) sugar and 1 egg. Blend well.

Cream butter with remaining sugar.
Gradually beat in remaining eggs, then
vanilla and almond mixture. Gradually
fold flour and baking powder into egg
mixture. Spread in buttered 25×38-cm
(10×15-in) swiss roll tin. Bake 30
minutes. Allow to cool in pan. Cut into
small squares or diamonds.

Soften fondant in bowl set over a pan of
simmering water, stirring occasionally.
Pour into 3 small bowls placed in a basin
of hot water. Flavour with vanilla or
almond essence. Add colouring. Dip cake
pieces individually into fondant. Decorate
while still moist.

Makes about 40 petits fours.

BRANDY ROPE RINGS

250 g (8 oz/1 cup) butter, softened
155 g (5 oz/¾ cup) sugar
310 g (10 oz/2½ cups) plain flour, sifted
1 teaspoon ground cinnamon
3 tablespoons brandy

Preheat oven to 180C (350F). Cream butter and sugar together until light and fluffy. Stir flour and cinnamon into creamed mixture. Stir in brandy and mix well.

Turn dough onto a floured board and roll to ½-cm (¼-in) thickness. Cut dough into 2×13-cm (¾×5-in) strips. Twist two of the strips together to form a 'rope'.

Join the two ends of the 'ropes' together to form a circle. Repeat with remaining strips. Place circles on baking sheets lined with greaseproof paper. Bake 15 minutes or until golden brown. These biscuits can be left plain, drizzled with glaze or threaded together with ribbon. They can also be hung on the Christmas tree or boxed as gifts.

Makes about 24.

MINCEMEAT TARTS

250 g (8oz/1¾ cups) plain flour
1 tablespoon sugar
155 g (5 oz/⅔ cup) butter, chopped
2 tablespoons water
1 egg yolk, beaten
Mincemeat, page 63
Icing sugar, if desired

In mixing bowl, combine flour and sugar. Cut in butter until mixture resembles coarse meal. Add egg yolk and water and mix into a firm dough. Wrap and refrigerate 1 hour.

Preheat oven to 190C (375F). On a floured surface, roll pastry to ¼-cm (⅛-in) thickness. Cut into 8-cm (3-in) circles with plain or fluted edge cutter. These are for bottom crusts. For top crusts, cut dough into 4-cm (1½-in) rounds with plain or fluted edge cutter. Place bottom pastry circles into pans. Fill with a heaping teaspoon of mincemeat. Cover with top pastry circles.

Using a fork, pierce pastry circles to allow steam to escape. Bake 10 minutes, or until the tarts are a light golden brown. Place on wire racks to cool. Dust with icing sugar if desired. Store in an airtight container up to 3 days.

Makes about 10 tarts.

CHRISTMAS CRACKERS

2 tablespoons Cointreau or orange liqueur
60 g (2 oz/½ cup) slivered almonds
1 kg (2 lb.) Mincemeat, page 63
8 sheets of filo pastry
60 g (2 oz/¼ cup) butter, melted
4 tablespoons dry bread crumbs
1 egg, beaten
Red and green maraschino cherries, small silver dragées
(silver balls), for decoration

Preheat oven to 230C (450F). In a bowl, mix Cointreau, almonds and mincemeat together. Lay a sheet of pastry on a board, brush with melted butter. Sprinkle with 1 tablespoon bread crumbs; cover with another sheet of pastry, brush again with butter.

Spoon a quarter of mincemeat mixture into a long roll 4-cm (1½-in) in from the long edge, leaving 9-cm (3½-in) from short edges. Cut short edges of the pastry using pinking shears, if desired. Roll pastry enclosing mincemeat, gently twist ends. Make 3 more rolls in the same manner.

Place crackers on a baking sheet lined with greaseproof paper. Roll 8 small balls out of foil 1.5-cm (½-in) in diameter. Place a ball in each end of each cracker to hold pastry open. Brush crackers with beaten egg. Bake 10 minutes, or until pastry is golden brown. Cool on a wire rack. To decorate crackers, arrange red and green cherries and small dragées attractively on top.

Makes 4 crackers.

CHRISTMAS GARLAND

125 g (4 oz/½ cup) butter
185 g (6 oz/1½ cups) sifted, all-purpose flour
2 tablespoons caster sugar
60 ml (2 fl oz/¼ cup) lemon juice
1 egg yolk, and extra for glazing
2 to 4 tablespoons water
125 g (4 oz/¾ cup) blanched almonds
60 g (2 oz/⅓ cup) candied lemon peel
60 g (2 oz/¼ cup) sugar
1 egg white
Few drops of almond essence
1 teaspoon grated lemon peel
20 red and green glacé cherries, chopped
60 g (2 oz/½ cup) icing sugar, sifted
2 teaspoons lemon juice, warmed
Nuts, glacé cherries and candied peel, to decorate

In a large mixing bowl, cut butter into flour and caster sugar until mixture resembles coarse breadcrumbs. Mix in lemon juice and egg yolk. Add water to form a firm dough. Wrap; refrigerate 8 hours. Roll dough to a large rectangle.

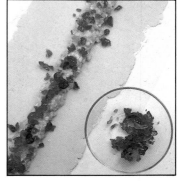

In a food processor or blender, combine next 6 ingredients. Cover; refrigerate 8 hours. Roll into a long sausage, place down the centre of dough. Sprinkle filling with cherries. Brush edges of dough with water. Fold over filling to form a roll. Press together firmly.

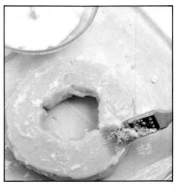

Gently shape roll into a circle, pressing the open ends together carefully. Place seam-side down on greased baking sheet. Brush with egg white. Refrigerate 30 minutes. Preheat oven to 200C (400F) 20 to 25 minutes, or until golden brown. Cool. Mix icing sugar and lemon juice. Drizzle over garland. Decorate.

Makes 1 garland.

FRUIT CAKE

250 g (8 oz/1½ cups) whole Brazil nuts
250 g (8 oz/2 cups) walnut halves
125 g (4 oz/1 cup) whole blanched almonds
125 g (4 oz/¾ cup) mixed candied peel
125 g (4 oz/¾ cup) chopped stoned dates
125 g (4 oz/¾ cup) chopped raisins
60 g (2 oz/¼ cup) glacé or candied ginger
250 g (8 oz/1¾ cup) plain flour
½ teaspoon baking powder
105 g (3½ oz/½ cup) caster sugar
3 eggs, lightly beaten
Few drops vanilla essence
Glacé cherries, for decoration

Preheat oven to 125C (275F). Line a buttered 23 x 13-cm (9 x 5-in) loaf tin with greaseproof paper. Butter greaseproof paper well. Place nuts, candied peel, dates, raisins and ginger in a large bowl. Reserve some nuts to decorate top of cake. Sift together flour and baking powder. Add to fruit and nuts and mix in sugar.

Stir in eggs and vanilla until thoroughly combined. Pack into loaf tin.

Decorate top with reserved nuts and glacé cherries. Bake 2 to 2½ hours, or until fine skewer inserted into centre comes out clean. Allow cake to cool for ½ hour in loaf tin before turning out onto wire rack to cool completely. Store in an airtight container – will keep up to 12 months.

Makes 1 (23×13-cm/9×5-in) loaf.

SIMNEL CAKE

900 g (2 lb.) mixed dried fruit, such as raisins, apricots, prunes, figs or dates; chopped
125 ml (4 fl oz/½ cup) sherry or brandy
2 tablespoons orange marmalade
250 g (8 oz/1½ cups) brown sugar
5 eggs
250 g (8 oz/1 cup) butter, melted
250 g (8 oz/2 cups) self-raising flour
450 g (1 lb.) marzipan for icing

Scour and dry terracotta pots 10–12-cm (4–4½-in) across the top. Line pots with well buttered foil, set aside. Preheat oven to 140C (275F). In a bowl combine chopped dried fruit with sherry. Allow to marinate at room temperature for 4 hours. Combine marinated fruit with marmalade, brown sugar, eggs, butter and flour.

Divide mixture evenly between four pots. Place all four on large baking sheet. Bake 2 hours or until skewer inserted into centre comes out clean. Allow the cakes to cool in pots. Invert then remove foil. Roll ¼ of marzipan between two sheets of wax paper to ¼–½-cm (⅛–¼-in) thickness. Cover top of each cake. Roll remaining marzipan into balls. Place on top of cakes.

Makes 4 cakes.

PASSOVER NUT CAKE

4 eggs, room temperature
220 g (7oz/1 cup) sugar
Pinch of salt
450 g (1 lb.) Brazil nuts, or walnuts, finely ground
Coarsely chopped nuts for decoration

Preheat oven to 180C (350F). In a large bowl, beat together eggs, sugar and salt until they are a pale lemon colour, thick and fluffy.

Fold finely ground nuts into egg mixture.

Pour into a lightly oiled 20-cm (8-in) round cake tin. Decorate top with coarsely chopped nuts. Bake 45 minutes to 1 hour. Let stand 10 minutes before turning out onto a cake rack to cool completely. During Passover this cake is not iced. However, a chocolate glacé icing is nice.

Makes 1 (20-cm/8-in) cake.

SEEDED BREAD STICKS

1 tablespoon dried yeast
125 ml (4 fl oz/½ cup) warm water
4 teaspoons honey
125 g (4 oz/½ cup) butter, chopped
1 teaspoon salt
125 ml (4 fl oz/½ cup) water
1 egg, beaten
440 g (14 oz/3¼ cups) plain flour
1 egg
½ teaspoon water
Caraway, sesame and poppy seeds

In a small bowl, mix together yeast, warm water and 1 teaspoon honey. Set aside and allow yeast to become foamy. In a saucepan, combine butter, **remaining 3 teaspoons honey, salt and water.** Heat gently until butter and honey melt. Pour liquid into large warmed bowl. Add beaten egg and yeast to mixture.

Beat in flour. Do not knead dough. Cover and place in refrigerator until cold. Divide dough into 12 pieces. On a floured board, roll each piece to a **30-cm (12-in) length. Cut in 2 to form 2 even lengths. Place lengths on greased baking sheet about 10-cm (4-in) apart.**

In a small bowl beat remaining egg with 1 teaspoon water. Brush egg mixture over dough lengths. Sprinkle with seeds. Let rise in a warm place 30 minutes or until not quite doubled in size. Preheat oven to 220C (425F). Bake 15 minutes, or until golden brown. Cool on a wire rack.

Makes 24 sticks.

A selection of savoury cheeses garnished
with fruit. Clockwise from the top:
Cheese and Walnuts, page 39; Goat
Cheese in Olive Oil, page 36; Spiked
Cheese Balls, page 37.

A tempting array of delicious snacks.
Stuffed Cherry Tomatoes, page 40;
Bridge Canapés, page 42.

A delightful combination for a lunch-
time snack. Clockwise from the top:
Seeded Bread Sticks, page 119; Pickled
Mushrooms, page 26; Rillettes, page 56.

An assortment of delectable sweets.
Clockwise from the top:
Chocolate Dipped Strawberries, page 86;
Chocolate Truffles, page 96; Petits Fours,
page 111; Marzipan Fruits, page 84;
Coffee Liqueur, page 75.

A charming combination for dessert.
Brandy Snap Basket, page 108;
Macedoine of Fruit in Brandy, page 72.

A range of savoury snacks and preserves
for the perfect ploughman's lunch.
Clockwise from the top: Pickled Mixed
Vegetables, page 24; Green Peppercorn
Mustard, page 16; English Pork Pie, page
58; Olive Cheese Balls, page 38; Pickled
Gherkins, page 22.

An appetizing variety of preserves and muffins. Clockwise from the top: Herb Muffins, page 100; Rum and Plum Jam, page 65; Rosemary and Quince Jelly, page 68; Apricot and Almond Conserve, page 62; Sultana Bran Muffins, page 101.

A selection of tasty appetizers.
Clockwise from the top: Green
Marinated Olives, page 35; Sweet Spiced
Nuts, page 33; Black Marinated Olives,
page 35; Mexican Peanuts, page 34.

INDEX

Apricot And Almond
  Conserve, 62, 126
Apricot Balls, 81

Basil Butter, 21
Biscuits, Raspberry Hazelnut,
  106
Biscuits, Walnut And
  Chocolate, 107
Black Cardamom Olives, 35, 127
Blueberry Or Blackberry Jellies,
  78
Blue Cheese Dip And
  Crackers, 44
Blue Cheese Dressing, 8
Bran Crackers, 45
Brandied Peaches, 70
Brandy Rope Rings, 112
Brandy Snap Baskets, 108, 124
Bread Sticks, Seeded, 119, 122
Bridge Canapés, 42, 121
Butter, Basil, 21
Butter, Garlic, 21
Butter, Mixed Herb, 21
Butter, Rum, 73
Buttered Brazil Nuts, 92
Butters, Herb, 21

Canapés, Bridge, 42, 121
Caramelized Fruits, 85
Cheddar Cheese Crackers, 44
Cheese And Walnuts, 39, 120
Cherry Tomatoes, Stuffed, 40,
  121
Chicken Liver Pâté, 51
Chilli Nuts, 32
Chilli Oil, 20
Chilli Sauce, 13
Chinese Chicken Wings, 47
Chocolate Boxes, 110
Chocolate Covered Prunes, 87
Chocolate Dipped
  Strawberries, 86, 123
Chocolate Fingers, 104
Chocolate Icing, 94, 107
Chocolate Liqueur Shells, 97
Chocolate Logs, 93
Chocolate Truffles, 96, 123
Christmas Crackers, 114
Christmas Garland, 115
Coffee Liqueur, 75, 123
Conserve, Apricot and
  Almond, 62, 126

Dipping Sauce, 46
Dressing, Green Goddess, 9

Easter Eggs, Ice Cream, 98, 99
Easy Chocolate Fudge, 94
English Herb Vinegar, 19
English Pork Pies, 58, 59, 125

Figs In Brandy, 69
Fish Pâté, 50
Flavoured Oils, 20
Florentines, 109
Frittata, 43
Fruit Cake, 116
Fruit, Spiced Dried, 80
Fudge, Easy Chocolate, 94
Fudge, Mocha Nut, 95

Garlic Butter, 21
Garlic Oil, 20

Ginger Beer, Old Fashioned,
  74
Ginger Biscuits, 105
Goat Cheese In Olive Oil, 36,
  120
Grand Marnier Pâté, 52, 53
Grapefruit Marmalade, 64
Green Coriander Olives, 35,
  127
Green Goddess Dressing, 9
Green Peppercorn Mustard,
  16, 125

Herb Butters, 21
Herb Muffins, 100, 126
Honey and Apricot Spread, 61
Horseradish Mustard, 17
Hot Malt Whisky Mustard, 18

Ice Cream Easter Eggs, 98, 99
Irish Cream Whisky, 76

Jam, Rum And Plum, 65, 126
Jellies, Blueberry Or
  Blackberry, 78
Jellies, Kiwi Fruit, 79
Jelly, Mint, 28
Jelly, Rosemary And Quince, 68,
  126
Jelly, Sage And Apple, 29

Kiwi Fruit Jellies, 79

Lemon Curd, 60
Lemon Drops, 88
Liqueur, Peppermint, 77

Macedoine Of Fruit In Brandy,
  72, 124
Marinated Olives, 35, 127
Marmalade, Grapefruit, 64
Marzipan Fruits, 84, 123
Mayonnaise, 10
Mexican Peanuts, 34, 127
Microwave Strawberry Jam, 67
Mincemeat, 63
Mincemeat Tarts, 113
Mint Jelly, 28
Mixed Currant Jelly, 66
Mixed Herb Vinegar, 19
Mixed Toffees, 91
Mixed Vegetables, Pickled, 24,
  125
Mocha Nut Fudge, 95
Muesli Bars, 103
Mushrooms, Pickled, 26, 122
Mustard, Green Peppercorn,
  16, 125
Mustard, Horseradish, 17
Mustard, Hot Malt Whisky, 18

Neapolitan Tomato Sauce, 14
Nuts, Buttered Brazil, 92
Nuts, Sweet Spiced, 33, 127
Nut Toffees, 90

Old Fashioned Ginger Beer, 74
Olives, Black Cardamom, 35,
  127
Olive Cheese Balls, 38, 125
Olives, Green Coriander, 35,
  127
Olives, Marinated, 35, 127
Oils, Flavoured, 20

Onions, Pickled, 25
Orange Peel, Sugared, 83

Passover Nut Cake, 118
Pâté, Fish, 50
Pâté, Grand Marnier, 52, 53
Peach Chutney, 30
Peanuts, Mexican, 34, 127
Pearl Balls With Dipping
  Sauce, 46
Pears Stuffed With Gorgonzola,
  41
Peel, Sugared Orange, 83
Peppermint Liqueur, 77
Petits Fours, 111, 123
Piccalilli, 27
Pickled Gherkins, 22, 125
Pickled Mixed Vegetables, 24,
  125
Pickled Mushrooms, 26, 122
Pickled Onions, 25
Pickled Watermelon, 23
Pork And Veal Terrine, 54, 55
Potted Salmon, 49
Prunes, Chocolate Covered, 87
Prunes In Rum, 71

Raspberry Hazelnut Biscuits,
  106
Rillettes, 56, 122
Rosemary and Quince Jelly, 68,
  126
Rum And Plum Jam, 65, 126
Rum Balls, 82
Rum Butter, 73

Sage And Apple Jelly, 29
Salmon, Potted, 49
Salsa Bolognese, 12
Salsa Pizzaiolo, 14
Scottish Shortbread, 102
Seafood Dip, 48
Seeded Bread Sticks, 119, 122
Simnel Cake, 117
Spanakopita, 57
Spiced Dried Fruit, 80
Spicy Apple Chutney, 31
Spicy Barbecue Sauce, 11
Spiked Cheese Balls, 37, 120
Strawberries, Chocolate
  Dipped, 86, 123
Stuffed Cherry Tomatoes, 40,
  121
Sugared Orange Peel, 83
Sultana Bran Muffins, 101, 126
Sweet Spiced Nuts, 33, 127

Tarragon Vinegar, 19
Toffee Apples, 89
Toffees, Mixed, 91
Toffees, Nut, 90
Tomato Relish, 15
Truffles, Chocolate, 96, 123

Vinegar, English Herb, 19
Vinegar, Mixed Herb, 19
Vinegar, Tarragon, 19

Walnut And Chocolate
  Biscuits, 107
Watermelon, Pickled, 23
Whisky, Irish Cream, 76